HE BROUGHT ME OUT!

Eunice Porter

Dear Judy,
You are such a bright spot in this world, and I am so glad I have come to know you. God bless you as you live for Him!

Love
Eunice

2 Peter 1:2-4

xulon PRESS

TABLE OF CONTENTS

STUDY TWO: A NEW WALK

STUDY THREE: A NEW SONG

PREFACE &
ACKNOWLEDGMENTS

$\mathcal{H}$ ave you ever asked yourself as a Christian if you are really living in the joy, peace and love of the Lord? Do you sometimes feel like the Israelites, wandering in the wilderness, bored, restless, unhappy, unfulfilled, depressed or sickly? That was me, in the Spring of 2010. About eighteen months previously, I had surgery for colon cancer, and was still dealing with the effects of now having only a 'semicolon'. Alternate methods of healing were not helping, and at the same time, it seemed as if my spirit had dried up within me. It was like being in a deep, slimy pit, with no way out. This concerned me, but I didn't know what to do about it. I had no desire to pray, or read God's Word, and yet kept up the charade by going to church, and pretending to be 'spiritual'.

One morning after church, a friend approached me, and said, "God told me to come to church this morning and give you this book." That impressed me, because the idea of God actually telling people what to do in everyday life was a bit 'out there' in my thinking. I accepted the book from her, and started to read. My fundamental theology began to be challenged, but soon I was asking, "Where has this teaching been all my life? This is exactly what I need! Why haven't I been taught these truths from God's Word? Why am I wandering in the desert when I could be enjoying the blessings of the Promised Land?" The teaching was really nothing new – it was there in the Word all the time, but overshadowed by emphases on themes more pleasing to the ears. After all, who wants to be told there might be things in our lives (hidden or blatant) that could be causing us to experience a disconnect from God and others, even from ourselves, and bringing mental anguish and physical ailments into our lives?

What I really appreciated as I continued to read, was that there was an answer to this dilemma. It wasn't long before I found myself repenting with bitter tears for things the Holy Spirit was revealing to me about myself – my wrong thinking, my bad attitudes, un-forgiveness, fear, the lies I was living, my past sins, and even the sins of my generations! It wasn't just saying, "I'm guilty". It was taking responsibility for, and turning away from those things, casting them out in the name of Jesus. Peace, relief and joy immediately followed each renouncement, as I asked for and received the complete forgiveness of the Father of Love. He had been waiting for so long for me to reach out and receive His grace and mercy.

The book I am referring to, and which has had a profound impact on my life, was written by a pastor who believes that God wants His people to be well, as evidenced by many words devoted to this theme in Deuteronomy 28, and statements like "He forgives all your iniquities and heals all your diseases" (Psalm 103:3) and "by His stripes we are healed" (Isaiah 53:5; 1 Peter 2:24). Years of study of God's truth, and medical research into the factors behind most illnesses went into the book, "A More Excellent Way to Be in Health", by Pastor Henry Wright. God has used these teachings on "spiritual roots of disease" to restore to health many who had lost all hope of cures through conventional or holistic means.

Most importantly people have been brought back into fellowship with God, and healthy relationships with others and themselves. I am just one of thousands who are living proof of God's desire and power to heal and restore, through repentance and sanctification.

I need to acknowledge, and I do so gladly, that the book "A More Excellent Way to Be in Health" was the springboard for what I have written in the following pages. I did not intend in any way to 'rehash', restructure, or embellish what Pastor Wright has said. I invite you to visit the website at beinhealth.com, and watch the Online Conferences by DVD (ten teachings of thirty minutes each), to get an introduction to this life-changing message. I shall be eternally grateful that he persevered against much opposition from various sectors, so that his book could be placed in my hands. I also want to thank all who have encouraged me on my walk-out to wellness, through the Be In Health program.

As I began writing a book based on my own story of rescue and restoration, it was not my intention for it to be some sort of autobiography, or a saga of my personal journey. I just knew that God wanted me to share what He has been teaching me. As it progressed, it seemed to take on the characteristics of a Bible study, with a lot of scripture references to explore, rather than a quick-read, quick-forget (?) style. With this in mind, it has been divided into three distinct but consecutive and related themes, each with thirteen chapters (suitable for seasonal Group studies). There are no leaders' guides or questions, which I have found from personal experience can take away from what the Word is actually teaching, and lead down useless rabbit trails. I trust my words will encourage you to let the Holy Spirit take His word and open your mind and spiritual eyes to life-changing truths you may not have seen before.

Dedication

I dedicate this book, with prayer, to you who are

'sick and tired',

'at the end of your rope',

hurting from past wounds,

broken hearted,

feeling hopeless, depressed or lonely,

feeling distant from God,

defeated, fearful, or oppressed,

looking for love, joy and peace,

stressed out and struggling,

desire the abundant life Jesus promised;

and to all who care about hurting people,
and want to help them.

STUDY ONE

"OUT OF THE MIRY CLAY"

Psalm 40:2

1

WHO ARE WE? AND WHY DO WE DO WHAT WE DO?

"In the beginning" – a good place to start, right? God (Father, Son and Holy Spirit) was there in the beginning, but this was not <u>His</u> beginning. With our finite thinking, it's really not easy to wrap our minds around the concept of eternity, that God always was, and always will be – the I AM of Exodus 3:14, of John 8:58 and of Revelation 1:8. This eternal Godhead was the thought, the word and the action that brought into existence the limitless universe that it would take eternity to explore – all held together by the word of His power! (Hebrew 1:3). As awesome as that is, God focused in on one infinitesimal part of His creation, spending time and putting careful creative thought into fashioning a perfect home for His final and ultimate work of creation. Then, when everything was in place - a world full of exquisite sights, sounds and creatures - He created <u>man</u> in His own image, forming him from clay, and breathing into his nostrils the breath of life; and man became a living soul – with a mind to think, a will to choose and emotions to feel. We

(mankind) have been created with the ability to think, speak and act, reflecting our likeness to the Godhead. But, more than that, like the Godhead, we are three-part beings. God's breath, His spirit, was breathed into us, so not only can we communicate with others through our soul part, we can communicate with God through the spirit part of us. We are spiritual beings, with a soul encased in a body. (1 Thes.5:23 and Heb.4:12) WOW!

In one paragraph, we have the condensed version of who we are! But we all know we are very complex and unique individuals in every aspect of our being – no two of us exactly the same, and yet all bearing the image of God. We were created 'special', apart from all other creatures. In Psa.139:1-18, David expresses, with wonder and amazement, how unique and precious we are to the God Who made us with such intricacy and detail, His love displayed in every cell and gene. Because we received His breath of life, our spirits hunger for Him, even as He longs for us to fellowship with Him. Really!! And this takes us to the next question, as to why we do what we do.

Because Adam and Eve were spiritual beings, God, who is Spirit, was able to talk with them in their beautiful garden. For the same reason, Satan, also a spirit being, was able to talk to Eve, tempting her to listen to his lies, and to doubt God. Satan accessed Eve's soul (mind, will and emotions) through her spirit. The lies entered her mind, and probably made her a little angry with God for apparently holding out on her. It seems she got excited at the idea of becoming like a god, knowing good and evil; and she willed to disobey God's command and instead to believe and act on the lies of Satan. Adam followed suit, and immediately, for the first time ever, they were both filled with fear, guilt and shame. They sewed fig leaves together to try and cover their shame. They hid, because they now feared the God they had come to love and trust. Finally, they tried to assuage their guilt by shifting the blame for their actions onto someone else. The fellowship was broken, their spirit separated from God's Spirit by sin. And the rest is history. Paul writes in Romans chapter five:

- v.5 "through one man sin entered the world, and death through sin, and thus death spread to all men"
- v.17 "by the one man's offense death reigned"
- v.18 "judgment came to all men, resulting in condemnation"
- v.19 "by one man's disobedience many were made sinners".

The nature of mankind was tainted by sin, the nature that was passed down through every generation since Adam.

Not much has changed since that fateful day in Eden – Satan is still feeding us his lies. He is, after all, the father of lies (John 8:44). He's got the whole world system under his influence – but, he knows his time is short for doing his destructive work. He realizes that he was defeated when God, the Son, shed His untainted, precious blood to destroy the power of sin and the works of the devil, crushing Satan's head under his heel, as foretold in Genesis 3:15. To 'get back' at God, Satan has made it his goal to destroy the works of God by causing God's children to sin. He is helped in this by the fact that many followers of Jesus don't give him any credence, not realizing we are called to spiritual warfare against this enemy of our souls (Eph.6:10-12). We have armor and weapons provided by the Captain of our salvation (Eph. 6:13-18; 2 Cor.10:4), and authority in the name of Jesus to cast him out. (Luke 10:19; Mark 16:17). (We need to know he was defeated, not banished – he keeps doing his dirty work!)

15

Yes, like it or not, Satan is still around, and we, God's people, are his prime target. As Jesus said, (John 10:10) he comes to steal, kill and destroy the sheep of God's fold – that's us. (See 1 Peter 5:8). How can he do this? He steals our health, kills our joy, and destroys our witness, etc., etc. – just plain keeps us miserable and defeated. As with Eve, he feeds lies into our mind, so that we think they are our own thoughts. He hopes that, like Eve, we will agree with his thoughts and doubt God; that we'll be filled with fear instead of faith, and with the works of the flesh instead of the fruit of the Spirit. (Gal.5:19-23). He can come masquerading as an angel of light (2 Cor.11:14), so if we are not grounded in God's Word, and cannot discern between the spirit of truth and the spirit of error, we can be easily deceived and turned from the path of God (1 John 4:1). Satan loves to take advantage of our hurts and wounds and lack of knowledge to bring us into anger, self condemnation and fear, and all the things that keep us bound and defeated. He wants to replace the blessings of God in our lives with his 'blessings', which are really curses (Deut.28:15-68). Many of the diseases in our body are caused by the effects of fear (Luke 21:26), lust (Prov.7:21-23), envy (Prov. 14:30), etc. in our soul. As our misery increases, then Satan accuses us and condemns us about the very things he has brought into our lives, making us even more miserable (Rev.12:10). What's wrong with this picture? I think you agree that it's not at all a 'pretty picture'. When we are miserable, 'he's laughin', and when we are joyful, he's miserable. Guess which scenario is pleasing to God!!

So, what to do??? How do we get out of the snares of the devil? How do we live the way God wants us to live? Where is the abundant life Jesus promised? (John 10:10b). Why can't I control my thoughts? Why do I feel so depressed? Why do I have so much fear? Why do I worry so much?

Why am I sick? Why doesn't God heal me? What is the answer? I hope that you, dear reader, are serious about your faith in Christ, and about following Him in obedience. If this is true of you, and you are asking some of these questions, read on – there IS hope.

2

DOES GOD HAVE AN ANTIDOTE FOR MY FEARS?

rom the story of the first parents we have seen that our faith can be replaced by fear, and this can result in our lives being ruled by fear. There are about 4,000 known fears to choose from – fear of failure, fear of tomorrow, fear of disease and death, fear of man, fear of facing our past, fears over finances, fear of relationships, even fear of food, just to name a few. In today's world, fear is known as stress/anxiety, and this is recognized in the medical world as the reason for any number of diseases. Does God want us to live in fear and worry, or does He want us to live by faith in Him to protect, provide for and heal us? (Matt.6:31-34) <u>God</u> has not given us the spirit of fear (Rom.8:15; 2 Tim.1:7), so if we are filled with fear, we can be sure it's a curse of the devil, to deter us from depending on God, to keep us defeated, to bring us disease and depression, doubt and double-mindedness.

2 Timothy 1:7 tells us God has not given us a spirit of fear, but of '<u>power, love, and a sound mind'</u>. Herein is the 3-fold antidote to fear – the triune God Himself. The Holy Spirit is the <u>power</u> – the power that raised Jesus from the dead –

this is the power God has given us to overcome fear. So it comes down to whose voice we are listening to and obeying – Satan's voice that tells us that God can't be trusted to care for us; or the voice of God's Spirit that tells us we have His authority to cast out fear, and that we can trust God implicitly. The Holy Spirit gave us new birth into God's family. He brought us out of the kingdom of Satan and of darkness, into the kingdom of God and of Light (Col.1:13). He brought us into <u>faith</u>, not into <u>fear</u>. God has placed His Spirit in our hearts, and wants us to know peace rather than fear. Are we in fellowship with the Holy Spirit, listening to His voice? Or is His voice silenced, and His power quenched by the sins of fear, doubt and unbelief?

The second cord in the fear antidote is <u>love</u>. Who is love? God, the Father! (1 John 4:16 and John 3:16) We talk of God's love, we sing of God's love, but do we really know our Father's love, and experience it personally? (Eph.3:17-19). God's Father-love toward us is perfect, complete and unconditional. He loves every human being, because that is His nature; that is Who He is. He has a special love for His children, those of us who have accepted His Son as our Savior from sin and death. He wanted so much to adopt us into His family as sons and daughters that He was willing to give His beloved Son over to death, to be made a curse for us, in order to remove the curse of sin from our lives, and pour His love into our hearts. (Rom.5:5) It is this perfect 'Father' love that casts out fear. (1 John 4:18) When we really know the Father's love, accept and appropriate His love, and live in the warmth and shelter and provision of the Father's love, how <u>can</u> we, or why <u>would</u> we have any fear? (Zeph.3:17). Your Father wants to spend time with you. He wants to whisper His words of love in your ear and into your heart. He wants to carry your burdens and heal your hurts. He wants to protect and provide for you. He wants you to come to Him at any time, with all your problems and needs, and your joys. (His door is always open!) Romans 8:15 tells us "you did not receive the spirit of bondage again to fear, but you received the Spirit of adoption, by whom we cry out 'ABBA Father'" (Papa Daddy). As your dear 'Daddy' He wants to give you so many things out of His great store of gifts! Don't live like a pauper in the Father's house!

Don't let fear, guilt or shame keep you from our Father's love. He knows all about you – He sees that fear, that guilt, that shame. He knows the hurts and wounds in your soul. He sees the bitterness, the pride, the self-pity - and He loves you anyway. But He grieves that you don't recognize and repent of all these things that keep you from His love and fellowship. He knows that all these 'respectable sins' break our fellowship with the Godhead, with other people, and even with ourselves, because we want to hide those things, and try to forget they are there. God is waiting in love for us to accept His love and forgiveness. Think of the story of the prodigal son in Luke 15:11-23. How long he lived in misery before remembering his father loved him, and returned home, to find that his father was waiting, running to meet him with open arms, gifts and a party! When we truly know God's love experientially, we will love Him, we will love others, and we will love ourselves. We will be able to accept <u>ourselves</u>, because we now understand that <u>God</u> loves and accepts us.

The third component of the antidote to fear is a <u>Sound Mind</u>. A sound mind speaks of sanity, clear thinking, focus and wisdom. It is <u>not</u> confusion, inner conflict or foolishness, double mindedness or depression. It <u>is</u> the renewed mind referred to in Romans 12:2. How are our minds renewed? By the Word of God! Jesus is that Word, sent by the Father into this world, as a man. Here, on the planet that He created by His word, He spoke His words of truth to listening ears and hearts. Today, God, the Word, wants to renew our minds, to sanctify us through His truth – His Word is truth – He is truth (John 17:17-19). Jesus wants His thoughts to be our thoughts. Philippians 2:5 says, "Let this mind be in you that was in Christ Jesus" – a mind so saturated with His thoughts, that it is actually His mind in us (1 Cor.2:16). Christ, the Word, is the sound mind that God has given us. A renewed mind does not happen instantaneously, or automatically, nor can we divorce the Word from the Holy Spirit, who gives us a hunger for the Word, brings it alive to us, and gives us understanding so we can assimilate its truths into our lives. Thus our souls are nourished, and our minds are renewed.

Do you suppose that in a sound, renewed mind there is room for fear? NO! Conversely, if we listen to, or watch, or think about things that feed fear, lust, greed and violence, or open the door to the occult, we block and hinder the ability of the Holy Spirit to renew our minds through the Word. Are we going to obey the Holy Spirit, or the gods of this world? Do we want to be conformed to the world, or transformed by the renewing of our mind? Do we want to live the abundant life, free of fear, guilt and shame? Or will we keep striving in our own strength to control our wicked thoughts; medicating our pain and our moods; hiding behind that 'smiling face' mask on Sunday morning? Are we going to stay in that horrible pit, stuck in the miry clay? Or will we let God bring us up out of that pit, set our feet on a rock, establish our steps, and put a new song in our mouth – even praise to our God? (Psalm 40:2-3 - Read the whole Psalm!)

3

SHALOM THROUGH SANCTIFICATION

G od talks a lot in his Word about sanctification. Don't let the length or unfamiliarity of this word scare you off. It simply means being set apart for a specific purpose or person. In the context of New Testament teaching, we, the children of God, are to be set apart to God, for His purposes, and for His glory. This includes not only being set apart to God, but also set apart from sin, the world's system and values, and the works of our former soulish life (often referred to as the old nature, the carnal nature or deeds of the flesh). Sanctification is accomplished as we put off these old habits and deeds, which are not fitting for a child of God, and which grieve the Holy Spirit if we continue in them (Eph.4:22). In tandem with this, our minds need to be renewed (Rom.12:2, Col.3:10, Eph.4:23) as we put on the new man, that new creature God made us in Christ (Eph.4:24, 2 Cor.5:17). Sanctification is not immediately accomplished when we initially become a child of God through the new birth by the Spirit of God. It is the process of holiness and the path to purity.

It is decidedly God's will that we be sanctified. He did not bring us out of the kingdom of darkness so we could bring all the trappings of that kingdom with us into our new kingdom of light, and continue to live under their influence and control. The key word here is 'continue', because, while we <u>all</u> bring baggage from our old life into the new life, we are to <u>change</u> our behavior, our thoughts, and our beliefs. The tragedy is that most of us don't know how this happens. Years, and even decades after we step into the new life, we are still harboring deep within us (and sometimes not so deep as to be undetected by others), wrong beliefs about ourselves and about God, lies from Satan that have brought unforgiveness, bitterness, fear, self-condemnation, pride, unbelief, and other crippling 'junk' into our souls. Many of these things are a result of hurts from the past, which we have never resolved or released. They eat away at us, affecting our mental state, and our physical health. Not only that, but they make us ineffectual for the kingdom of God and His work in and through us. This all to emphasis our <u>need for</u> this thing called sanctification.

The change that needs to come <u>does not</u>, and <u>cannot</u>, be accomplished in our own strength, or by our will power. In fact this only compounds the problem, as another dead work is added to the list of undesirables in us. When Jesus prayed to His Father for His disciples, He said, "Sanctify them through Your truth. Your word is truth" (John 17:17). Just minutes earlier, he had told them that when He went back to the Father, He would send the Holy Spirit to be with them forever (this promise includes us!), and that this "Spirit of truth will guide you into all truth." What does this mean for sanctification? Simply put, as we hear, read and meditate on the word of God, the Spirit of God in us (see Rom.8:9), that same Spirit who inspired the word to be written, will use the truths of the word to reveal the things in us that need to be excised (Heb.4:12-13). But are we indeed listening to His voice of conviction? Please note that His conviction is not to bring us into self-condemnation, or any other kind of condemnation, but to an awareness of the sin, so that we can repent of it, renounce it and cast it from our lives – in the name of Jesus, who through His death on the cross, paid the debt of our sin, and provided forgiveness for all our sin. All we need to do is accept that forgiveness. (The voice that speaks condemnation into our minds, is the voice of that old accuser of the brethren to put us under more condemnation – this is the voice that we need to reject, and close our minds to, while keeping our minds tuned to the frequency of God's Spirit, through fellowship with Him in His word and prayer.)

All of this tells me that God hasn't changed. He still hates sin (not the sinner – He loves us, sin and all – Rom.5:8). AND, He wants us to be pure and blameless. After all, we are the bride of Christ! (Eph.5:25-27) Sounds pretty easy so far, right? Did you come across the word 'repent' in the previous paragraph? The fact is, it is the desire and work of the Holy Spirit to sanctify us; but He needs our co-operation – not our works, and not our efforts. We actually play a part in the process, and it's so easy, and so freeing, that it is like play, not work. In a word, our part is to 'repent'. Repentance is our path from bondage to freedom. Just to clarify, repentance is not doing penance, it's not making restitution, and it's not even making longs prayers of lament and pleas for mercy. We'll address the meaning shortly, but first, we need to see what an important word this is in God's vocabulary – and should be in ours!

From John the Baptist's call for repentance in the book of Matthew (ch.3:2), to John the Apostle's message of repentance to the seven churches in the book of Revelation, (2:5, 16, 21; 3:3, 19), the New Testament alone is filled with the command to REPENT! I emphasize this, not to negate the fact that it occurs even oftener in the Old Testament, but to show that it is relevant in the New Testament, and therefore for <u>us</u>. The following verses about our need to repent are found in the epistles, written to the church (that's us!) Rom.6:11-13; Rom.13:12-14; 2 Cor.7:1; 9-10; Gal.6:8; Eph.4:22; 25-31; Col.3:5-10; 1 Thes.5:22; 1 Tim.6:10-11; 2 Tim.2:24-26; Tit.2:11-14; Jas.3:14-16; Jas.4:8; 1 John 1:8-9

God knows the connection between sin and sickness. (He made the rules – Deuteronomy 28:15-68) And He knows that repentance of sin and obedience to His Word brings blessing and <u>peace</u>, which in turn brings health (Deut. 28:1-14). This is expressed in the word 'shalom', the Hebrew word translated 'peace' in the Old Testament. According to Strong's Concordance (7965), it includes "completeness, wholeness, health, peace, welfare, safety, soundness, tranquility, prosperity, perfectness, fullness, rest, harmony, the absence of agitation or discord". This is all found in Jesus, the Prince of Peace, and it is God's plan for all His children. But, again, I say, He needs our co-operation. He did not foist Salvation on us, and He doesn't give us His peace unless we are willing to receive it on His terms. Imagine telling God, "I don't want your peace. I want to continue living in torment, and fear and guilt, because I am not willing to give them up. That's just who I am. So, no thanks, I'll pass"! When you think about it, that's exactly what a lot of His children are saying, really!

4

JOYFUL REPENTANCE?

*W*hen we honestly ask the Holy Spirit to search us (Psa.139:23-24), and show us our sin, He will convict us of the things He sees, not to condemn us, but to allow us to recognize, and take responsibility for listening to Satan's lies and making them a part of our life. We need to recognize it as sin, and confess it to God, receiving His forgiveness. (Confession is agreeing with God about our sin – in other words, admitting it). But we also need to repent. (There's that word again!) Repentance is not just saying, "Oops, I did it again!" It's having a revulsion and abhorrence of our sin, and renouncing it, turning away from it, and forsaking it, making a 180 degree turn in the opposite direction. True repentance is often accompanied by tears of sorrow, at having grieved God's heart by harboring the sin, and by refusing His forgiveness and cleansing. Remember, we are talking about the 'respectable' sins, like jealousy and greed, anger, taking offence, unforgiveness, etc. It is by the act of repentance that we are 'putting off the deeds of the body' which are contrary to the mind of God, in order that the robe of Christ's righteousness which God has clothed us with will no longer be covered by the stains of sin and the rags of self-righteousness, but will shine forth to the world with the purity God wants us to walk in every day (Col.3:10).

The act of repentance includes receiving forgiveness, not just for sins we overtly commit, but for things that are not of God which we are entertaining in our mind; i.e. wrong thinking, attitudes and beliefs that keep us from embracing God's truth. There is nothing too insignificant or too terrible for God's forgiveness. How long has He been waiting for you to accept His forgiveness and cleansing? It is yours, just for the asking, and accepting. As we receive His forgiveness, relinquish and renounce these sins, and cast them out from us in Jesus' name, the sorrow and tears of repentance suddenly are changed into joyful tears of release, and lightness and freedom! The next time the enemy whispers into our mind that we should react to someone's words with anger, malice or self-pity, we can "bring that thought into captivity to the obedience of Christ" (2 Cor.10:5), and tell that liar, Satan, to get lost. This, in part at least, is what it means to resist the devil. As we remind him, and ourselves that we are forgiven through Christ's blood, he flees from us.

Both Peter and James address this issue in the New Testament. 1 Peter 5:6-9 says we are to humble ourselves under God's hand, and cast all our cares on Him (this looks like repentance and relinquishing to me!); we are to be watchful, because "your adversary, the devil, walks about like a roaring lion, seeking whom he may devour. Resist him, steadfast in the faith." Through our position in Christ by grace through faith, we have authority over the devil, in the name of Jesus. (Luke 10:17-19) We are to resist him and send him packing! This good news is also found in James 4:7-8. Note the correct order: 1) "Submit yourselves to God" (see verse 6), then 2) ''Resist the devil, AND HE WILL FLEE FROM YOU"! Included in submitting to God is what we talked about earlier – coming into fellowship with the Godhead - Father, Son and Holy Spirit, so that we can always draw on His love and truth and power –weapons that Satan cannot stand against. Verse 8 of James 4 indicates that drawing near to God requires a purity of mind, body and spirit – the result of repentance.

In our lives as children of God, we are not to fight against people – even when they attack us. Our warfare is against the kingdom of Satan (Eph.6:12). Our weapons are not physical and tangible, but powerful spiritual weapons and armor provided to us by our God, who is well acquainted with every tactic and scheme and weapon of Satan. (2 Cor.10:3-5; Ephesians 6:11-18) The battle is against the enemy that has set up camp in our minds! But, we have learned how to wield our spiritual weapons against him. We need to remind him, and ourselves, that his game is up. He's defeated already, and he can't fool us into thinking we're powerless to fight him off. We have renounced him, and annulled any right for him to order us around, or camp on our property. A reminder to us: W*hen we entertain his thoughts, meditate on them, and let them become part of our thinking, it is then that we give him a legal right to be there!*

We don't need to fear Satan and his army of demons, first of all because he is already a defeated foe, and also because the Holy Spirit in us is greater than he is (1 John 4:4). Satan shudders and cowers and slinks away at the name of Jesus, and cannot abide in the presence of the truth revealed to us by the Holy Spirit. Knowing this and acting on it is vital for victory. Don't listen to the enemy – you will soon learn the sound of his voice and can shut him up and slam the door in his face before he finishes his thought. Remember, YOU have the authority to do this in the name of Jesus. Don't argue with him, either. Talk to him, and tell him to leave now in the name of Jesus. Speak in an audible voice, and with authority. Maybe he needs to be reminded that you have repented of that sin, and been forgiven, and he has no right to bring it up, or accuse you of it again (Unless you have been taken in by his wiles once more – so, you repent again). Incidentally, repentance is not a once for all, 'now I'm done, now I'm perfect, and I'll never have to repent again' scenario. Neither is it onerous! It's the joyful and quick way back into the Father's fellowship, and into freedom and peace.

As we cleanse ourselves from the 'besetting'/'ensnaring' sins, and the spirits of fear, bitterness, rebellion (also called witchcraft - 1 Sam.15:23), and any number of others, through repentance, then comes the renewing of our mind through the Word by the Holy Spirit, replacing those old thought patterns based on lies, with new thought patterns based on the truth. This is the TRUTH that sets us free! (John 8:32) Self-condemnation is gone, as we realize our true worth in Christ, as children of God. Guilt and shame have to leave, because innocence and confidence are restored. (1 John 3:21-22). Fear is banished by love, and replaced by faith in God. Instead of greed and envy and jealousy, we are content, and can rejoice in the blessings and successes of others. Hatred and resentment towards our abusers turns to love, and the wounds no longer hurt, because we have forgiven them. (We are able to separate the sinner from the act of sin, because we recognize that person was a tool of Satan to try and destroy one of God's precious ones.) (See our example for forgiveness in Luke 23:34).

5

NOTHING HIDDEN

*I*t is very possible that we are harboring within us generational sins (iniquities), such as a spirit of lust, murder, or lying; of inherited disease, occult influence and so on. (Exod.20:5) The very nature of some of these inherited vices demands secrecy, so we may not even be aware that they exist in the family tree, and yet they manifest in our lives from generation to generation. Does anyone identify with this? Maybe you have horrible thoughts, or recurring nightmares, or evil desires that you can't explain, and that make you think you're crazy, or at least incredibly 'bad'! Just as Nehemiah (Neh.9:2) and Ezra (Ezra 9:6-7) repented for the sins of corporate Israel , and for the sins of their forefathers, sometimes we need to repent on behalf of our ancestors, for *their* sins, in order to break the curse of their iniquity in our lives, and in the lives of our children, and the generations to come. You can stop the iniquity now, bringing release and freedom for yourself and those who follow you. Is that Good News, or what?

Sometimes, the evil in us is buried so deep in our being, hidden under layers of excuses, rationalization or denial, and we have erected such protective strongholds around it, that it may take years for the layers to be peeled away, or the walls demolished, to reveal it, *unless we become proactive in this sanctification process.* How can we do this? First of all, don't be a navel-gazer, or be looking under every stone for a demon. And don't get someone to analyze you to try and figure out what your problem is. (This is not what a warrior does. A good soldier does not act on his own, but is always submissive and obedient to the command of his Captain.) Secondly, we need to accept the fact that God knows us, inside out, and, to quote Hebrews 4:13: "There is no creature hidden from His sight, but all things are naked and open to the eyes of Him to whom we must give account". Knowing this, and that whatever might be hidden is not beyond God's grace to forgive, nor His power to heal, we need to pray for God to shine His searchlight into those hidden places (Psa.139:23-24), to reveal to us what has been concealed and maybe forgotten for years, and to prepare our hearts for repentance, whether it seems too small and insignificant a thing to bother with, or too horrible and degrading to look at. Again, let me say, this is not to make you relive what you have tried so hard to forget. It is to get that deadly demon rooted out, as God leads you through repentance to forgiveness. This gives you freedom to forgive someone who hurt you, to forgive yourself for the shame and guilt you feel, and if necessary to forgive God for any resentment or anger you have felt towards Him. It also allows for deep wounds to be healed, and for your soul to be restored. What freedom and joy comes as we submit to God, for His searching, cleansing, and restoration, as we take back what the enemy has stolen from us for far too long! Truly we experience what David wrote in Psalm 40:2-3. The good news just keeps on coming!

It's time to let God have control of every part of us (Romans 6:13, 19; 12:1). It's past time for us to yield to and cooperate with the Holy Spirit to allow Him to do that spiritual house-cleaning that will make us pure, and ready for Him to use to fulfill the purpose God has for us from the foundation of the world. Are you ready to accept and act on these truths today, or are you satisfied with the status quo? Here are a couple of quotes I heard recently, but cannot recall the source:

"There's no value to seeking more truth until we are obedient to the truth we already know."

"Truth only becomes of value to us and changes us as it travels from our thinking to our being. We can't just chew on it and then spit it out. It must be assimilated and become part of us."

The truth of what you have been reading (or hearing) herein is so well expressed in the words of 2 Peter 1:3-4: "His divine power has given to us all things that pertain to life and godliness through the knowledge of Him Who called us by glory and virtue, by which have been given to us exceeding great and precious promises, that through these you may be partakers of the divine nature, having escaped the corruption that is in the world through lust." This is God's will and plan for his people. Sadly, for many in our churches today:

✓ *We want the blessings without the obedience.*
✓ *We want the Promised Land, and we want the peace, but we also want to 'cohabit with the enemy', rather than to destroy his works and cast him out of our lives by the power of Jesus' name, and the authority of the Holy Spirit.*
✓ *We want the rewards of righteousness, without repentance from dead works, without renouncing and removing the hidden things of darkness in our souls*
✓ *We want Jesus to save us from the penalty of sin, while we continue to willingly live under sin's power,*

defeated and joyless. We sin with impunity, and wonder why we're miserable.

My friends, "These things ought not so to be"! As one who wandered in the wilderness for forty years and more, going in circles, and getting nowhere, but at last has entered the God-intended rest of His promised land, I implore you to think upon these things. Don't merely be hearers of the Word. Jesus is still saying to each one of us, "If you love me, you will keep my commandments." Do we love Him??

p.s. Speaking of the promised land, I understood for many years that the land of milk and honey promised to God's people, Israel, was, for the church, a type of heaven. Looking back, I can see how erroneous that thinking is. God miraculously delivered Israel from their oppressor, as He has, through Christ, delivered us from the kingdom of Satan. At the threshold of Canaan, fear of the enemy, due to their unbelief (disobedience), kept them from entering 'their rest'. For forty years, a whole generation wandered in the desert, dying one by one, never realizing the blessings God had for them. (Deut.28:1-14.) People of God, why are we wandering in the desert? Why haven't we entered *our rest* (Heb.4:9-11), and claimed our possessions in Christ? (Hebrew 3–4). Instead of believing that as we go in faith, God will fight the enemy for us, that He has already won the victory, and will hand us innumerable blessings, we retreat from Satan in fear, letting him rob us of everything God intended for us to enjoy. My dear friends, this is SO NOT the Abundant Life! Do we need to repent firstly, of our fear, unbelief, wrong theology and disobedience? God have mercy on us!

6

GATEKEEPERS

*W*hen we hear the word 'walls', we may envision a
building, or a structure around something of value,
to protect it. Walls keep out what is undesirable, and keep in
what we treasure. Where you find a wall, you will find doors
or gates, the vulnerable parts of the wall, where an unwel-
come intruder may gain entrance, killing the occupants and
stealing or destroying their goods. The Bible talks a lot about
doors and gates, about doorkeepers and gatekeepers. When
God set up His tabernacle among His people in the wilderness, the tent-like structure meant that its walls could be
easily dismantled for travel, and thus they were extremely
vulnerable. In Numbers 1:50 and 53, we are told that members of the Levites, the chosen priestly tribe, were appointed
to care for all the precious furnishings of the tabernacle, and
to "camp around the tabernacle" to keep out what was unholy,
and protect what was sanctified inside. Many generations
later, Solomon built the temple, to replace the tabernacle.
It was a house with strong walls, filled with costly articles
of worship, and with the glory of the Lord. Again from the
Levites, this time four thousand men were appointed, not to
camp around the temple but to be gatekeepers, each assigned
a gate, and a season of service. (See 1 Chron. 23:4-5, and

26:1-19.) (In the interim, certain Levites were assigned to be gatekeepers for the ark – 1 Chron.15:18, 23-24). All these gatekeepers had an awesome responsibility, to guard the treasures from defilement and destruction due to unlawful entry by what was unclean.

As we look through the succeeding history, we can't help wondering what happened to the gatekeepers. When Josiah was king of Judah, and ordered repairs on the temple, Hilkiah, the high priest found the Book of the Law in the temple. When the king heard the words of this book, he repented for his sins, and covenanted to follow the LORD, and keep His commandments. He ordered the priests and the doorkeepers to cleanse the temple – 2 Kings 23:4-7. How had these idols and images of heathen gods and nature worship found their way into God's house? The gatekeepers had been derelict in their duty, so the temple of God was defiled with corruption! Think ahead to the cleansing of the temple by Jesus. Had the gatekeepers been so blinded by greed to allow these money-changers and animals into the temple court? (John 2:13-16) Going back to the time of Ezekiel, God showed this prophet, by means of visions, the unthinkable abominations the people of Israel were committing in the temple – idol worship, obscenities, immorality, and defilement, that literally drove God out of His sanctuary (Ezek. 8 to 11). Where were the gatekeepers? And, generations later, when Ezra and Zerubbabel with some fifty thousand other Jews returned to Jerusalem from the Babylonian captivity, to find the temple in ruins, completely destroyed, where were the gatekeepers? In the midst of much opposition from their enemies, the temple was restored, but was not in any way as glorious as it had been. In God's faithfulness the temple furniture and articles that had been robbed by the armies of Babylon, was restored and brought back to where they belonged in the temple. (God is still in the business of taking back from the enemy what he has stolen from God's people!)

What does any of this have to do with me, or the church, here and now? When Cain brought an unacceptable offering, God reminded him that he would be accepted if he did well. If he didn't do well, sin was crouching at the <u>door</u>, and desired to have him, but he should have the rule over it. By letting jealousy and anger stay in his heart, Cain's mind was over-powered by that crouching sin, and he slew his brother. The Apostle Paul reminds us that in order to win over the enemy of our souls, we need to "bring every thought into captivity to the obedience of Christ."(2 Cor.10:5) In other words, if a thought enters our mind that is not in obedience to Christ, that thought is from the enemy of our souls, so instead of entertaining it, (letting it in and listening to it), we must reject it, replacing it with the truth of Christ. <u>We</u> are gate-keepers over the temple of God who dwells in us. We must recognize the enemy, and refuse him access to our minds and hearts. The only one we are to allow access to is the Holy Spirit. See John 10:2-3. As gatekeepers we are to "keep our hearts with all diligence, for out of it spring the issues of life" (Prov.4:23). Just as nothing unclean was allowed in the temple, but only what was sanctified, so we are to keep our hearts pure. (James 4:8; 1 Pet.1:14-16; 2:1-2) What are we allowing into the temple of our mind through the ear-gate and the eye-gate? What and whom are we listening to, that defiles our mind? What are we watching when no one is watching us? Even things we touch and taste can lead to sin – remember Eve? 2 Cor.6:17 says, "Do not touch what is unclean". And how many men are captured by sin through smelling a certain perfume? Don't be deceived by Satan's lie that "If it feels good, it's okay"! As people of God, redeemed from sin by the precious blood of Christ, we are no longer to be sensual (driven by our senses), but spiritual, under the control of the Holy Spirit, set apart to Christ, the members of our body yielded to God as instruments of righteousness (Rom.6:13)

What do we do when the Holy Spirit shows us that in the deep hidden parts of our soul there is rubble, and refuse and wickedness, just as was the case in the temple of old? The idols must be torn from our hearts, and our souls must be surrendered to the Holy Spirit, the only legal occupant of the heart of a child of God. Only then will true worship be restored in God's temple, God can restore what Satan has stolen from us, and we will be filled with His glory, which will shine out to the world like a beacon, beckoning sinners to the Light of the world.

As individuals, we are gatekeepers, guarding the treasure of Truth and Life within us. Pastors and church leaders are also gatekeepers standing as sentinels and watchmen at the door of the sheepfold to protect God's treasure (the people of His pasture and the sheep of His hand – Psalm 95:7), recognizing and keeping out the enemy (1 John 4:1-6), and letting in Jesus, Who by His abiding presence and work, tends and cares for His sheep, giving them the abundant life He promised in John 10:10. These words were spoken by the Good Shepherd Himself (John 10:11-18). Pastors, be faithful gatekeepers, and let the true Shepherd nurture His flock, and bring other sheep into His fold. Consider your calling as a gatekeeper to be a great privilege even as the psalmist did who wrote Psalm 84:10-12. Amen!

7

OUR OWN WORST ENEMY

$\mathcal{H}$ as anyone ever told you that you are your own worst enemy? I realize that I have been focusing a lot on the fact that Satan is our enemy. He is called this in Matt.13:39 and Luke 10:17-19. 1 Pet.5:8 refers to him as our adversary, seeking to devour us like a roaring lion. In the Old Testament record of Israel, one of the first orders from God upon entering the Promised Land was to rout out and destroy the wicked inhabitants of Canaan, in order to cleanse the land of defilement. This 'enemy' is a picture of Satan who is an adversary, not just of God's people, but of God Himself. He delights in ensnaring and crippling us through sin and disease, to keep us from living the abundant life, and from being God's lights and witnesses to a dark world. Whenever he touches one of God's children, he is hurting God (Zech.2:8).

Often, however, <u>we</u> are sabotaging the work of God in our lives, playing into the hand of the enemy, self-destructing, and defeating our own purposes and desires to live a victorious Christian life. Yes, in many ways, we have become our own enemy. We are so busy fighting against ourselves that we are incapable of resisting our real enemy! How can this be, and why does it happen? In short, we have listened to

Satan's lies, (often spoken through people who should love us), that we are ugly, worthless, nothing but a burden; until we believe the lies, and become our own enemy. Let me say that this is *not* God's will. Eph.6:12 says we do not wrestle against *flesh and blood* – humans, including ourselves. <u>We are not our enemy!</u>

Do you ever say, "I hate myself!"? The word for enemy comes from the Greek word 'to hate'. If God loves you, and He *does*, He wants you to love yourself. Jesus once said, "Love your neighbor as yourself" inferring that you can't love anyone else unless you first love yourself. (and implying that other people are not our enemies either!) So how can we change? Ask God to pour out His love into your heart by His Holy Spirit (Rom.5:5). Pray the words of Eph.3:16-19 over and over, until you understand in the core of your being how much your heavenly Father loves you. Picture yourself in His arms - close, happy, safe. Listen to His words of love in the songs He sings to you, and the plans He has for you as His special child. Then you will be able to love yourself, and be your own friend. You will find that as you learn to love yourself, by accepting God's love, you will be able to love others, and others will love you.(John 13:34) Give yourself a hug, smile at yourself in the mirror, and speak only the words that encourage and uplift yourself as a child of the Most High God that you are! And tell God how very sorry you are that you have harbored the sins of self-hatred, self-rejection, self-accusation and all the other self-destroying things in your life. Accept His forgiveness, and walk with your head high in the knowledge of who you are in Christ.

One of the ways God has shown His love is by giving us His Holy Spirit to live in our spirit, to teach us, guide us, comfort and help us (John 14:16-18,26). He never intended that we try to live as His child on our own. We accept the fact that we cannot save ourselves – that it is all of God's grace, as we accept the gift of His Son, who died in our place for the forgiveness of our sin. We understand that our new birth was a work of the Holy Spirit to make us children of God. But, so often, like the Galatian believers, we check the Holy Spirit at the door of the nursery, and set out to live our lives without Him (Gal.3:3). This is the recipe for defeat, failure and despair. Read Gal.4:6-7 to see God's design for you. (Also see Gal.5:1, 16; 22-23). When will we start believing that God's plans for us are so much more wonderful than anything we can concoct? When will we seek the filling and anointing of the Holy Spirit, and continuously yield our mind, will and emotions to Him? Then our mourning will turn to joy, and the spirit of heaviness will give way to a spirit of praise. The broken places will be rebuilt, and the ruins restored (Isa.61). It's time to do yourself a favor, for the glory of God, and for His blessing on you!

We sabotage our joy and peace as a believer (and this is HUGE), if we believe that there is no enemy, that Satan cannot deceive us with his lies, and cannot bring doubt and fear or lust or bitterness into our soul. This is exactly what he wants us to think. He doesn't want us to face the wounds, hurts and sins of the past that have wreaked havoc on our emotions, and our health, physically and mentally. He wants us to keep building up the strongholds that guard the shameful secrets of our heart. He doesn't want us to know that iniquities and curses of past generations are affecting us and our children with all sorts of maladies and syndromes. He wants us to blame God for our problems, and seek relief from the broken cisterns of the world, that cannot help or heal. He hides our minds from the truth that God is our healer (Psa.103:2-5; Exod.15:26; Isa.53:5). He's happy that the church is full of hurting, sick and depressed people, and that the pastors have no answer for these ills, except to refer their sheep to the ravenous wolves of this world's systems, that rob, kill and destroy. It's time for the church to return to its mandate, operating in the gifts and power of the Spirit, preaching the doctrine of repentance and sanctification, spiritual warfare and victorious living. It's time for all of us as God's people to begin the journey back into fellowship with the Godhead. This needs to start by asking the Holy Spirit to show us the hidden sins of our heart, so that through repentance, forgiveness, deliverance and obedience, these noxious weeds will be rooted out, and we will find healing, restoration, and renewal of our mind. Only then will we be able as Christ's followers to proclaim the Gospel, and on His authority to heal the sick and cast out demons, in the power of the Holy Spirit.

There are many warnings in the Bible about being overcome by the world, and giving in to the lusts of the flesh. The pressures to conform to the thinking of the unregenerate mind, and partake of the ungodly works of the un-redeemed are subtle, sinister and unrelenting. Every time we turn on any of a number of electronic devices, our minds are in danger of being bombarded and defiled by degrading images and corrupt ideas, dressed up to appeal to our senses. There is NO way we can walk in the light of the new life in Christ and still walk in the darkness of this evil world. Don't sell your birthright for a bowl of stew as Esau did! "Choose this day whom you will serve." (Josh.24:15). Choose LIFE!

<u>8</u>

<u>BLESSINGS - PROMISES FOR OBEDIENCE</u>

❧

"I have set before you life and death, blessing
and cursing; therefore *choose life,*
that both you and your descendents may live"
- Deut.30:19

*G*od did not make us to be robots, or puppets on a string. He gave us the gift of choice, which has never been revoked. In God's economy, the choices we make determine our destiny. God is telling us here, and in the whole of Deut.28 as well, that if we commit to loving God, walking in His ways, and diligently obeying His voice, He will give us a life filled with multiple blessings. Conversely, if we turn away from Him, and disobey Him, death and curses will dog our steps. Who would want death and curses rather than life and blessing? So the real choice is: "Am I going to love and obey God, or disobey Him, and reject the life He offers?" Choosing *not* to obey is to choose an existence filled with curses instead of blessings.

If you ever have any doubts as to whether it's worthwhile to follow Christ, read, and re-read Deut.28:1-14. Think about the words of 1 Tim.6:17:"The living God ... gives us richly all things to enjoy", and Prov. 10:22:"The blessing of the LORD makes one rich, and He adds no sorrow with it". This is God's plan and desire for you, His child. All this, and heaven too! If you cannot fathom how much God wants to bless His children, get a comprehensive concordance and look up every reference to God's promises of blessing, and pronouncement of His blessing on both Israel and the New Testament church. Indeed you will find that the Living God is a Giving God. The greatest evidence of this is the indescribable gift of His Son, to purchase our redemption from sin and the kingdom of darkness. God gives because He loves – that is His nature.

As we read through the passages in the Scriptures about God's gifts and blessings, we notice several truths:

1. While His blessings are freely given, we need to *accept* and *appropriate* them in order to benefit from them. An untouched, unwrapped gift is a rejected gift, and hence is useless to us. We will never enjoy its worth or meaning or blessing. Also, by refusing the gift, we are in fact rejecting the one who gave it to us.

2. God wants us to *ask Him* for His gifts and blessings! i.e. Matt.7:7-11; John 14:13-14; Jas.1:5-7 (He wants us to not only ask, but ask in faith, believing we will receive what we need.) His is the heart of a loving Father wanting to lavish on His beloved children the gifts of His storehouse, and the blessings of his wealth, ultimately making them the heirs of all He has (Rom.8:32; 15-17; Eph.1:11, 18).

3. Although there are blessings that God gives indiscriminately, such as rain, sunshine and physical life, some blessings are reserved *exclusively* for His chosen ones, be it the Israelites or His church. Many of the blessings He gave Israel in Canaan are pictures of the ultimate crowning blessings that have come through Christ, the fulfillment of the types and shadows of the Old Covenant. (Have you read the book of Hebrews lately?) Some blessings promised to Abraham, and to his spiritual seed, were only fully realized after Pentecost, when the work of the cross was completed, and the promised Holy Spirit came upon the Church (Acts 2; Gal.3:5-14).

4. God's blessings and promises of blessing, unlike His love, are often *conditional*. As we search the Word, we will find many different conditions, predicated in most cases with that little word 'if'. We have already seen that the blessings of Deut.28 will come only *if* His people obey His commandments, and walk in the ways of the LORD. Any other condition we may come across is basically the same as this one, just couched in different language. The similarity of these conditions proves once more that God does not change, nor do His standards of righteousness and holiness, which cannot be compromised. I am listing here some of the references to God's blessings and the conditions attached: Exod.19:5; Lev.26:3-13; Deut.8:18; Deut.11:18-28; Josh.1:8; 2 Chron.17:3-6; Isa.1:19; 2 Pet.1:2-11; 1 John 2:3-5.

Throughout the Old Testament, we see that again and again God withheld blessing from His people, not on a whim, or to be mean, but because they kept straying from the path of blessing. His heart yearned for them to return to Him, to seek His face and walk in the ways of peace and blessing that He laid out for them. He wanted to provide them with choice food, houses and lands, prosperity and good health,

victory over their enemies, and the spoils of their battles. He
wanted them to possess a bountiful land, which he handed to
them on a platter, with one condition. In order to receive all
His blessings, they had to drive out and destroy the wicked
inhabitants who had proliferated in number and abominations during the over 400 years since Israel and his sons had
left their promised possession because of famine, to seek
refuge in Egypt. God even promised that he would fight
their battles for them, if only they would do as He asked
them. To demonstrate this, He told them to march around
the walled city of Jericho once a day for six days, with the
priests leading the procession blowing trumpets; on the sev-
enth day to circle the city seven times, then give one final
trumpet blast. On this cue the people were to shout loudly.
As they shouted, they watched those huge walls crumble and
fall in on the city and its people.

It wasn't long before some of the Israelites decided to make
treaties and alliances with the evil nations of Canaan instead
of destroying them all – to intermarry with them, to worship
their idols. How soon they turned their backs on the God
Who had rescued them from the oppressive slavery of Egypt
with many signs and wonders; they forgot the One Who had
fed and cared for them in the wilderness, and brought them
to this beautiful land. And because this God still loved them,
He stopped the blessings they were no longer grateful for, in
order to let them recall the place from which they had been
delivered, repent of their sins, and seek His forgiveness. Is
there not a lesson here for us? Our heavenly Father loves us
SO much, and wants to shower us with His bounty of blessings. If we are not receiving and enjoying these blessings in
our lives, could it be that instead of driving out and defeating
the enemy of our souls, we have let him come into our lives
with his lies, filling us with fear, guilt and shame? Are we
still clinging to the sins of Egypt, and to the iniquities of

the past generations, to the curses of occultism and spiritist practices? What idols have we set up in our hearts? Let the Holy Spirit search your heart through the words of Eph.4:17-32, bringing you to repentance, forgiveness, restoration and God's blessing! Choose LIFE!

2

CURSES – JUDGMENT ON DISOBEDIENCE

"*C*hrist has redeemed us from the curse of the law, having become a curse for us." (Gal.3:13) Look back at v.10, which, by quoting from Deut. 27:26, explains what the curse of the law is. This same curse is reiterated in Deut.28:15 as well as in vs.45-47 and vs.58-61, amid the pronouncement of specific judgments against disobedience of God's commandments. (Read Deut.28:15-68). These judgments are the curse of the law – all manner of disease, blight, oppression, suffering, want, and destruction, etc. To this day we understand that if you break the law, there will be punishment. (Note: Laws protect us *only* if they are obeyed!) The first curse/judgment was pronounced against the serpent after he tempted Eve to disobey God. Up to that point, there was only blessing in the Garden. When Satan caused Eve to sin, he brought a curse upon himself, upon the land, upon Adam and Eve, and all the succeeding generations. (Gen.3:14-19). God, who is <u>good</u>, created mankind to enjoy His blessings, but the enemy, Satan, who is the epitome of <u>evil</u>, wants us to experience cursing instead of blessing.

The reason there is so much sorrow and destruction in the world is simply because most of humanity is under the dominion of Satan, living in the kingdom of darkness. Jesus, God's Light, came into the world to rescue mankind from this evil domain. Strangely, rather than come to the light, most reject it. (John 1:4-5; 3:19; 8:12) Why? Because their deeds are evil, and light exposes this. What is even stranger is the fact that there are many within the family of God who are living under these curses of sin in their lives, and are unwilling to let the searchlight of God expose the darkness in them so He can free them. For example, depression, heart attacks, all kinds of cancer, mental disorders, learning disabilities, digestive problems, chronic pain - do any of these conditions occur in God's children today? Do these maladies sound to you like blessings? NO, never. These are curses!

God is not malicious, handing out curses indiscriminately onto His people. Wherever there is a curse of this type, there is a reason behind it. It may come simply as a result of defiling or abusing our body, God's temple. It could also be that we are disobeying God by not honoring our parents, or the husband does not take his rightful position as spiritual leader and head of the home. Often there is a generational iniquity that has brought a spirit of lust, infirmity, bitterness, anger or shame into our souls. Traumas can wreak havoc in us as well, to cause all kinds of physical or mental distress and disease. As mentioned before, as a defense mechanism, generational iniquities and traumas are often buried and forgotten; but their roots keep growing down, and their branches keep growing up, until the 'fruit' manifests somehow in our behavior, and often as a sickness, mental unrest or an addiction. If you think about it, all sorts of problems can result from being rejected, unloved, or not properly nurtured as a child. We can allow a spirit of bitterness to enter us, if we feel someone has wronged us. Even imagined slights can damage our psyche, leaving us twisted in our thinking, miserable, hurting and sick. Is this really God's plan for you? (Jer.29:11-13)

Every one of these events in our lives, and in the lives of our ancestors gives the enemy, Satan, an open door to our soul, to plant his lies, to tell us we're going to get cancer because our father died of it, or that we are doomed to Alzheimer's just like our mother was. He tells us we are to blame for the abuse we were subjected to, and makes us feel fear, guilt, and shame. He plants in our mind the seeds of unforgiveness, envy or offence against someone who wronged us, which leads to a spirit of bitterness taking root in our soul, to poison and bind us. (Acts 8:22-23; 2 Cor.2:10-11; Heb.12:15) It is a well-documented fact that the condition of the soul is an indicator of the health of the body, and can also affect our degree of prosperity. The Apostle John wrote in his third epistle, "Beloved, I pray that you may prosper and be in health, just as your soul prospers."(v.2) Does this mean that if your emotions are stable, your mind is full of positive thoughts, and you don't waffle in decision-making, that your body will be healthier and you are more likely to be successful in life, than if uncontrolled emotions, a worried, anxious mind and a weak will, are sending signals to the glands and hormones in your body to over or under-secrete? That's exactly what the medical world is finding out more and more to be the case, and that the effects on the body are devastating. This is the curse of the law – in reality the result of believing the lies of Satan, and entertaining wrong thoughts, manifesting harmful emotions and committing acts of disobedience to God's laws.

If you are constantly doing things you don't want to do, thinking thoughts that are shameful and condemning, or hurting yourself and others by out-of-control emotions, all the while professing to follow Christ, are you seeing some discrepancies in your life? Is it fitting for a child of God, redeemed by grace through the cross of Christ, to be living under the curse of the law? Take some time to look at Romans 6 and 7, especially ch.7:14-24, and see Paul's struggle with this issue. Paul recognized that he was dealing with condemnation of sins in his life – perhaps from the past, from generational iniquities, or even present offences, that needed to be rooted out through repentance, forgiveness and restoration. He realized, as we need to, that Christ won the victory over all our sin – past, present and future - and over Satan at the cross, obtaining our freedom from sin's power. We have to choose to surrender to the Spirit to live the life of Christ in us (Rom.8:1-2; 9-11; 13). James 4:7-8 adds to this that we also need to "resist the devil and he will flee from" us. Yes, in the Name of Jesus, and by the authority of the Holy Spirit in us, we can send the enemy packing! Remember 1 John 4:4 – "He (Christ) who is in you is greater than he who is in the world."

I opened this chapter with the words from Gal.3:13, that "Christ has redeemed us from the curse of the law, having become a curse for us....*Cursed is everyone who hangs on a tree*" (quoting Deut.21:23). When Jesus hung on the cross, this sinless sacrifice became defiled in His soul by every sin of all mankind. He also bore in His body all those curses of the law, listed in Deut.28:15-68 – every judgment for disobedience was meted out on Him. "By <u>His</u> stripes <u>we</u> are healed" (Isa.53:5; 1 Pet.2:24). Accept healing today from Him "Who heals all your diseases" (Psa.103:3; Exod.15:26). AMEN!

10

FROM CURSE TO BLESSING

꽃

*D*on't you love the way God brings something to us at exactly the moment we need it? The last two chapters were written over the past few days, and as I closed them off, I felt there was more to say. No doubt volumes could be written, and the subject would not be exhausted. This morning, my Bible reading was in 2 Corinthians, but as I finished, I flipped ahead a few pages, thinking about how much I was anticipating delving into the book of Galatians, the letter of liberty. Suddenly my eyes landed on the words of chapter 3:10-14, and I was riveted by a truth I had never before realized. This is the key to the theme of Galatians, perhaps the theme itself! More than that, it is the crux of the Gospel, which Paul so passionately defends, throughout his letters, before kinsmen and kings, and particularly in the epistle to the Gentile believers of Galatia. This is one of those nuggets God has hidden in His word – rare, precious – waiting to be mined out, then treasured and enjoyed by all His people. Have you read it? Do you see what I see? Let's explore its wonder together.

We looked briefly at verse 10 before, from the standpoint that *the curse* comes by failure to obey the law, and includes all the curses pronounced against the disobedient, particularly in Deut.28:15-68. The ultimate curse of the law is death. Notice, in Gal.3:10, the phrase "the works of the law". It's hard work to *know* all the demands of the law, let alone *keep* them without ever slipping. In fact, it's impossible. The most devoted and godly could not honestly say they kept even the first commandment. By Jesus' interpretation of the law, the *thought* of evil was as condemning as committing the *act*. Because the law came from the holy, perfect, and righteous God, its standards are high, unattainable by fallen humanity. Was it ever the purpose of the law to make us righteous in God's eyes? According to vs.11-12 of Gal.3, the law was given as a standard to live by, not to justify us before God. (Also see vs. 21 and 24). Paul goes to great lengths in Galatians as well as in chapters 2-4 of Romans to prove that the law can NEVER make us holy, or perfect enough for God's standard. All the law can do is condemn, never justify us. In condemning us, it shows us our utter sinfulness before a holy God, and throws us on God's mercy and grace.

Abraham lived before the laws of God were given to His people, and it was because he believed and trusted God that he was justified before God (Gen.15:6; Gal.3:6). Keeping the law has nothing to do with faith. It was never the plan of God to bring redemption from sin and darkness by means of the law. What He did plan was to provide a sinless substitute who would carry the curse of the law in His body on the cross, Himself becoming the curse, and rendering it powerless through His death.(Gal.3:13). No human being, (all tainted with sin through Adam), could satisfy the demand of the law for this required death. That is why God Himself implanted His seed in the virgin womb of Mary, performing a miraculous intra-uterine insemination of holy seed, bypassing the seed of human man which is defiled by sin. And so was conceived the sinless God-man, born as a man here on earth, to show us the Father God. They called Him 'JESUS', because He would save His people from their sins (Matt.1:21). His birth was foretold several centuries earlier in Isaiah 7:14. There He was called 'Immanuel', meaning "God with us". Galatians 4:4 tells us that at precisely the right time, in exact fulfillment of God's purpose, Jesus was sent to earth, "born under the law". Yes, Jesus, the Son of God, as the son of man felt the restrictions and the burdens of the law. He was subjected to temptation by Satan, to break the law for His own comfort and advancement (Matt.4:2-11). Yet, He did not sin, but used the words of the law to defeat the devil. Through the power of the Spirit of God within Him, Jesus was able to resist and put the enemy to flight. He knew this was the only way for any man to do this, and He was constantly focused on His purpose and destiny here on this earth, to make it possible for us, His followers, to have the power of this same Holy Spirit to defeat the enemy in our lives.

Jesus' purpose in invading history, to be confined by the time and space of mortal man, was first pronounced in Gen.3:15, in God's curse against Satan for bringing the defilement of sin into His beautiful creation. He said, "I will put enmity between you and the woman, and between your seed and her Seed; He shall bruise your head, and you shall bruise His heel." Hundreds of years passed before this happened. In the interim, God called out a people for His name, to whom He gave His holy laws of instruction for living. He dwelt among them to protect and guide them. He set up an elaborate system of sacrifices designed to show them His holiness, and that they were to worship Him with clean hearts. Every one of these sacrifices was a picture pointing to the true sacrifice who was still to come. Those who offered them were not forgiven because of any virtue in the blood of animals (Heb.10:4), but because of faith in the One Who was covering over their sins until the blood of the perfect sacrifice was shed for the sins of all mankind. Through this final sacrifice all people of faith in God's salvation would be proclaimed righteous before God. It's interesting that the Hebrew word translated 'atonement' suggests a covering over, placation, forgiveness, expiation, whereas the Greek equivalent, used in reference to *Jesus'* sacrifice, is from the word 'exchange', and means *to restore to divine favor, to make pure* (Rom.5:11-KJV).

I also found it interesting that when we are redeemed from the curse of the law, we inherit "the blessing of Abraham", not the blessing of the law! (Gal.3:14) Truth be told, the blessings of Deut.28:1-14 aren't really inherent in the law itself, but only in the keeping of the law (which totally agrees with the statement that the law condemns!) So when we are redeemed from the curse of the law, we're free from its condemnation. Look back at Rom.8:1-2, and compare this to Gal.3:13-14b. In both cases we see that:

1) Christ has redeemed us from the condemnation of the law.

2) This same redemption has brought the blessing of Abraham on us, of salvation through faith, not works.

3) Best of all, through faith we receive the indwelling of the Holy Spirit! I believe this is the real fulfillment of God's promise to Abraham: "in you all the families of the earth shall be blessed." "... through His Spirit in the inner man, that Christ may dwell in your hearts by faith" (Eph.3:16-17). This is the secret to obeying the law of God in our hearts, which in turn means we receive the blessings of Deut.28:1-14! It's a WIN-WIN situation, all of GRACE! Read Gal.3:2, 3, and 5 and receive the blessing!

11

RENEWING THE MIND

ॐ

Romans 12:2 - "do not be conformed to this world,
but be transformed by the renewing of your mind."

*I*t's one thing to '*change* your mind', but '*renew* your
mind' goes way beyond that. It results in *transformation*. That sounds like a *God* thing, something supernatural,
even miraculous. Perhaps, but only as much so as the orig-
inal creation of the mind. Exactly! Paul wrote the book of
Romans, (including chapter 12, verse 2), under the direction
of the Spirit of God (2 Pet.1:21), the creator *and* renewer
of the human mind. With God, it's perfectly natural – hard
though for us to grasp. Just a re*mind*er – the mind is part of
our soul, and connects to the brain in our body. What the
mind thinks is recorded by the brain, and a thought that is
repeated many times lays down a thought pathway in the
brain. It appears from much study and research that negative thoughts in the mind (or negative emotions) cause the
brain to produce negative chemical reactions in the body,
which produces illness (often because of under or over
secretion of hormones). The process is much too compli-
cated for *my* brain to understand, so this is a very simplified
explanation. From a spiritual view, it's important to see that

because we have been living in the kingdom of darkness, our minds have been programmed to believe the lies of Satan, that came through bad life experiences. We were trained to think thoughts such as "I'll never amount to anything","I'm to blame for the abuse I suffered", "Nobody could ever love me", "I hate her, and I'll never forgive her", "I'm so afraid, I can't even function", and so on, endlessly. These thoughts have formed deep pathways in our brain, and translated into malfunction in our physical body and mind. Is anyone identifying with this scenario??

When God steps into our life, and through His amazing grace transfers us out of the kingdom of darkness into the kingdom of His dear Son (Col.1:13) through the cross, change happens. As the truth of God's word begins to enter our mind, we start to think new thoughts, like, "God made me for His special purpose, and I have value", "It's not my fault I was abused. I don't blame myself anymore", "God loves me for *me*, freely and unconditionally", "I can forgive and love her, because of God's love and forgiveness to me", and "Fear is not from God. He gives me the Spirit of power, love and a sound mind. His perfect love casts out every fear". As we meditate on these truths day after day, our brain begins to create new paths of peace and tranquility, which become our established thought habits in just a few weeks. Meanwhile, since we are no longer going over and over those old paths of lies, they gradually disappear (become overgrown). The combined result of these two processes is:

1) The good thoughts founded on truth have replaced the bad thoughts based on lies, so the newly formed, healthy neurons in the brain are now sending signals to the body that it can start functioning the way it was meant to; the 'juices' start flowing properly, and Voila! Health, wholeness and well-being begin to be restored.

2) Because of the new brain patterns that have been established, the brain sends a message of calm and serenity back to the mind, telling it to start functioning the way it was originally created to work. Soon double-mindedness becomes a thing of the past; psychological aberrations disappear; clouds of oppression and depression are lifted; addictions are healed and clear thinking restored. In short the mind has been renewed, sans medication, sans therapy. I hope this very simplified explanation brings some clarity regarding the subject at hand. (Science was never my forte!)

I have heard the theme of the renewal of our mind expounded upon many times, and it usually was just an admonition to study, learn and meditate on the Word of God. Ephesians 5:25b-26 agrees, and I quote: "Christ...loved the church and gave Himself for her that He might sanctify and cleanse her with the washing of water by the Word". In Jesus' prayer recorded in John 17, he prays, "Sanctify them by Your truth. Your word is truth" (v.17). I think I made it clear how important the truth of God's word is in mind renewal. I want you to notice a word that appears in both of the above quotes. It's the word 'sanctify'. Put this together with the last part of Eph.5:26, and add v.27, "that He might present her (the church) to Himself a glorious church, not having spot or wrinkle, or any such thing, but that she should be holy and without blemish." Sanctification, as explained in a previous chapter, is a process of cleansing and purifying (This might be a good time to review). First of all, the Holy Spirit must be active in our hearts so that the truths of God's word are made clear to us, and become a part of our being and belief system, not just our thinking. We need to be hearing and obeying His voice, as He reveals sins in our lives that must be repented of and cast off. This is our part in the sanctification process (Eph.4:29-31; Col.3:8-10; Jas.4:8). It is up to us to deal with the roots of the negative, destructive thinking of the unrenewed mind. Unless the roots are destroyed (cast out), the washing by the Holy Spirit cannot complete the full work of making us holy and without blemish. The evil thoughts might be flushed out, but more will spring up from those unseen roots and defile us (Heb.12:15).

Take another look at Col.3:8-10; Eph.4:22 and Rom.12:1-2. The message here does not sound like a teaching on passivity, simply letting the Holy Spirit do what He wants to do in your life, with no input or co-operation from us. It is so clear that <u>we ourselves</u> are to put off anger, wrath, malice, blasphemy, filthy language and lying (Col.3:8; Eph.4:22). Why? Because, by our choice to accept God's gift of salvation, we have put on the new man (Col.3:10; Eph.4:24). Those things don't fit our 'new man', and it is our duty, and yet our choice to cancel their lease in our life, and boot them out in the name of Jesus. We can't fully follow Christ while still clinging to these besetting sins. (Heb.12:1; Rom.12:2a). It seems that the mouth is often one of the last of our members to be sanctified. (Read about the untamable tongue in James 3:2-16). Not for a moment should a person who is still full of anger, wrath and bitterness ever accept this as being normal for a renewed mind. Nor should words like 'holy crap', and other 'potty-mouth' epithets ('filthy language'), or the vain use of the Lord's name, such as 'Oh my God' (blasphemy) be heard on the lips of a new person in Christ, any more than lying should. I wonder why we feel we need to adopt this worldly jargon, when God says we are not to be conformed to the world (squeezed into its mold - Rom.12:2; I Pet.1:13-15). Rather, "Present your bodies a living sacrifice, <u>holy, acceptable to God</u>. Only as we surrender to the Holy Spirit can our mind be renewed! (Rom.12:1-2) Surrender today – He's waiting - and you will never regret it!

12

HOUSE CLEANING
❧

*T*his morning I woke up to a messy kitchen, a dining table cluttered with a week's worth of mail and bulletins, a laptop surrounded by Bibles, concordance and scattered notes (which sort of overflowed into various other areas), and no real will to tackle the problem. Several things came to my mind. It was easy to justify the obvious neglect, as I have been busy writing, and just didn't have time. I was glad that I live by myself, and don't usually have pop-in visitors. I hate untidiness, but sometimes it has to get in-my-face to remind me that clutter is worse than cleaning. If someone called to say they were coming over, I would be a whirlwind of flurry with a mission – to make my home presentable, so I wouldn't be embarrassed! (1 John 2:28) And I was reminded of something I had recently witnessed.

Have you felt at times that the testimony of God's working in another person is a lot more interesting and amazing than what you have seen Him do in you? That thought crossed my mind when my friend, whom I will call Benita, was wondrously delivered from years of spiritual bondage, which had almost destroyed her. God reminded me that the same amazing grace had worked in us both, and it was no more difficult for Him to free one than the other (Eph.2:8). Without His intervention in our lives, we are all without hope (1 John 5:12). I had never wallowed in the depths of depression that had gripped her, but I still had to be rescued from the clutches of Satan, in order to live as a citizen of God's kingdom of light (Col.1:13-14; 1 Pet.2:9).

When you are in the dark, like a blind person you stumble over obstacles, bump into things, get hurt, are afraid and feel vulnerable. You can't see what's coming against you, and have no defenses against it. You also don't see the mess and debris around you, or the dust and grime covering everything (John 11:9-10). What a difference when the shutters are opened and the sunlight bursts in! (1 Cor.4:5) Reality hits! What was hidden is now revealed. You can see what you tripped on, or bumped your head against. And that disgusting film on every surface – ugh! Now you look at all the stuff you've accumulated and think "It's garbage!" (Phil.3:7-8) You realize it's time to clean house. You have figured out by now that I'm really talking about things that need to be removed from our spiritual lives. This is true, but maybe there are physical things around us, and especially in our homes, that are detrimental to growth in the Spirit, things that need to be destroyed, or they will destroy us (2 Cor.6:17; 7:1).

We may have sentimental attachment to things from the past, which without our knowledge may carry a curse, or be connected with pagan religions, both of which can give unclean spirits access into our home and life. Even pieces of furniture, if associated with obscene or occultic activity in the past, can have an evil influence on us. It may be possible to break such curses in the name of Jesus, cast out any spirits of lust, witchcraft, occultism, etc., and then pronounce a blessing over the article. However, if it is an object such as an idol, or image used in worship, often collected on trips overseas, it needs to be destroyed (Acts 19:19-20). (In some instances, the person who made an article for the tourist trade may have put a curse on it). A person who has ancestors who were Free Masons, or belonged to any societies connected to Free Masonry, probably has some ancestral curses over their life. Some indications of this are insomnia, learning disabilities, depression, mental illnesses, death wishes, epilepsy, chronic lingering pain and illnesses (usually unexplained), and being accident prone. The same applies if you or your ancestors have dabbled in pagan religions, witchcraft, Ouija boards, astrology, and séances, etc. These are not harmless pastimes. If you or someone in your family has unexplained illness, ask the Holy Spirit to show you if there really is an explanation, which the father of all that is evil does not want us to figure out. We must not be ignorant of his devices (2 Cor.2:11).

Benita, even though she had been a Christian for several years, through wrong choices in her past had given Satan access into her life, and he seemed determined to absolutely demolish her. But God was protecting her, and brought light to dispel the darkness of night. He replaced her bondage with freedom, and turned mourning into joy (Isa.61:1, 3). The change was indisputably miraculous. In the process of deliverance, through repentance of sins and casting out of the evil spirits behind the sins, her soul was cleansed of stuff that had kept her imprisoned for years. As soon as the release came, she knew immediately in her restored spirit that she also had to get rid of 'junk' in her home that was connected to the evil kingdom from which she had been rescued. The bookcase was purged of every book that espoused or resembled New Age teaching; exercising books or tapes based on Eastern religions, such as Yoga, Pilates, Tai Chi and so on; horror stories, and crime mysteries; romance novels; self-help books that did not acknowledge God; tomes on philosophy and man's reasoning, in short anything that did not 'fit' in the life of a child of God. Her new guidelines were found in Philippians 4:8: We are to meditate on whatever is true, noble, just, pure, lovely, of good report, virtuous and praiseworthy. What we read is what we will think about, and what we think about can either defile or edify us. Have you examined your bookcase lately? Are there things you would hide if you knew Jesus was dropping in? Guess what – He already knows what you have (Heb.4:13). Ask the Holy Spirit to show you what to discard, and to guide your future purchase choices (1 John 2:15-16).

Another area my friend decontaminated was her CD/DVD collection. Hard rock music with its vulgar lyrics had to go. That's a no-brainer! Is listening to lewd word pictures any different from watching porn? Just a different gate is all. Allowing this smut to enter our mind when we should have the mind of Christ is unthinkable. It's a desecration and defilement of the temple of God. Will we continue to drink from the cesspools of the world with impunity? Know this: There are consequences! The same holds true for the computer and TV, which also felt the holy fury of my friend's fervor. It wasn't that long ago that "The Young and the Restless', with its flagrant display of immoral lifestyles, was deleted from my 'must watch' list, along with numerous crime shows. What are you watching on TV? You are in charge of the remote control. Use it wisely! What about your computer? Does it need to be cleansed? Are you accessing sites that defile and corrupt your thinking? You are the gatekeeper of your mind. Be vigilant! Don't give access to the enemy. Get busy with that delete button! (Heb.12:1) One click can make you a slave or be your first step to freedom. It's your choice!

13

ANTI-VIRUS PROTECTION

𝕾𝕰

F or days, I kept getting pop-up reminders on my computer that my anti-virus subscription was about to
expire. Finally I decided, with just two days remaining, that
I needed to take action. This meant I had to stop writing, and
focus on renewing my contract. I admit it was a relief to know
my computer was 'safe' for another year. I was thankful for
this, and began to think about our lives as believers, and all
the damaging elements and devices that are trying to hack
into our souls, to render us useless; and of the safeguards
built into our salvation to protect us against these 'enemies'.
As is the case with computers, it is the responsibility of the
owner to ensure the safeguards are in place and in working
order. And we also need reminders from time to time!

Any corrupting or infecting influence can be called a virus.
Medically, it 'infects cells and changes how they function, to
cause disease symptoms', everything from the common cold
and flu to HIV and Hepatitis C. Webopedia defines a computer virus as 'a program or piece of code that is loaded into
your computer without your knowledge, and runs against
your wishes'. They can also 'replicate themselves, and
damage or shut down a system by interfering with its opera-

tion or gathering private information'. This reminds me of the Apostle Paul's words in Rom.7:23-24: 'I see another law in my members, warring against the law of my mind, and bringing me into captivity to the law of sin which is in my members. O wretched man that I am! Who will deliver me from this body of death?" (referred to as the body of sin in Rom.6:6). From what I understand, behind every computer virus is someone with (usually) malevolent motives, like a hacker. A hacker 'accesses a computer by circumventing its security system' (John 10:1). Likewise, (See James 1:14-15) behind the sin virus that invades our souls, (and ultimately our bodies), is the father of sin, our enemy, Satan, who has evil designs to steal, kill and destroy us (John 10:10).

Another computer term, Spam, also reminds me of how Satan operates in the lives of humans by 'sending unsolicited bulk messages indiscriminately' into our minds. Recently, with the wrong click of a button, I unwittingly opened up my computer to a LOT of Spam emails. It was a bombardment against me and my computer, which I am still trying to fight off. Have you ever been spiritually blasted by the enemy's attacks? They come as thoughts of doubt, envy, offence, un-forgiveness, and revenge; or feelings of anger, rejection, fear, despair, etc. Unless the safeguards are in place to thwart and diffuse these assaults, we can go down in defeat, to the devil's delight.

When God put His plan of Salvation and Redemption in place, He knew that His enemy, Satan/the devil, was going to be incessantly at war against the saints with every nefarious, villainous ploy and scheme in his evil character. For this reason, He made sure that every possible safeguard was built in to His plan, in order to protect His people from this enemy they would encounter (1 Pet.5:8), and prepare them for an unseen yet very real spiritual warfare against the powers and principalities of darkness and wickedness (Eph.6:12). He began at the cross, when in fulfillment of Gen.3:15, Jesus, by shedding His blood, bruised Satan's head, a sign to us that he is a defeated foe already, and we need not fear him if we confess Jesus as Lord and receive forgiveness of sin. That's why Rev.12:11 says of the saints in heaven that "they overcame Him by the blood of the Lamb and by the word of their testimony". Jesus, by dying for sin, satisfied all the charges that our accuser, Satan, can ever bring against us (Rom.8:1). The "word of their testimony" is our confession of faith in Christ, based on the authority of God's word and the blood of the cross (Col.1:20). In reference to this, and our other safeguards and defenses, I am going to make a list (which is not in any order of importance and may not be exhaustive), and some scripture references for each, for your study:

- *The Holy Spirit – (when we listen to His voice, and obey, and do not quench Him by sinning – Eph.4:30-32) – John 14:16-17, 25-26; 16:7-8; Acts 2:4; 16:6-7; Rom.8:2, 10-11, 13, 15, 26-27; 1 Cor.2:9-13; 6:11; 12:7-11; 2 Cor.3:17-18; Gal.4:6-7; 5:16-17, 22-23; Eph.1:13-14; 2:18, 22; 3:16, 20; 5:9; 6:17-18; Phil.1:19; 2 Thes.2:13; 2 Tim.1:7, 14; Rev.22:17.*
- *The Blood of Jesus – Rom.3:24-25; 5:9; Eph.1:7; Col.1:14, 20; Heb.9:11-14; 1 Pet.1:18-19; 1 John 1:7; Rev.1:5; 12:11*
- *The Name of Jesus – Prov.18:10; Isa.9:6; Mark 16:17-18; Luke 10:17-19; John 14:13; 15:16; 16:23, 26; Acts 3:6, 16; 4:10, 12, 29-31; 16:16-18; Phil.2:9-11.*
- *The Armor of God (2 Cor.10:4-6; Eph.6:11) –*
  1. *Breastplate of Righteousness - Isa.32:17; 41:10; Mal.4:2; Rom.4:6-7; 5:18-21; 2 Cor.6:7; Eph.6:14; 2 Pet.1:1. 2)*
  2. *Shield of Faith – Rom.5:1-2; 1 John 5:4; Eph.3:11-12; 6:16; Jas.1:5-6; 5:15.*

3. *Girdle of <u>Truth</u> and Sword of the Spirit/<u>the Word of God</u> – (as we study, memorize, meditate on and obey it, we renew our minds) – Deut.18:18-20; Josh.1:7-8; Psa.1:1-2; 40:11; 119:9, 11, 92, 104-105, 114-117, 130, 133, 165; Prov.13:14; Luke 4:1-8; John 8:51; 17:17; Rom.12:2; Eph.4:23; 5:9; 6:14; Jas.1:21-25; 1 John 2:5.*

4. *Helmet of the <u>Hope</u> of Salvation (1 Thes.5:8) – Rom.5:5; 15:13; 1 Thes.4:13-18; Tit.2:11-13; Heb.6:19; 1 John 3:2-3.*

5. *The Gospel of <u>Peace</u> – Matt.5:9; John 14:27; Eph.6:15; Phil.4:6-7; Col.1:19-21.*

Re: Eph.6:18, I like what Dick Eastman writes in New Spirit Filled Life Bible to the effect that prayer is not really a weapon, or a piece of armor, but is actually fighting the battle, with the armor provided. Prayer is battle, as any prayer-warrior will attest to!

Are these safeguards in place in your life? They are all available, just for the taking and using. They are part of the great Salvation package, to get us out of the horrible pit and unstuck from the miry clay, so we can cross the river and possess the Promised Land of rest and plenty. There will still be enemies to conquer, so we must know how and when to use these resources. The more we practice, the more effective we will become in defeating the enemy and thwarting any future assaults. Let God set your unencumbered feet upon a rock, and fit you with shoes to walk with Him into your inheritance!

STUDY TWO

A NEW WALK

Psalm 40:2b

14

RESTORATION
AND RENEWAL

❧

*H*as God in His grace and mercy lifted you out of the horrible pit of past hurts and nightmarish memories? Has He set you free from the miry clay of anger, bitterness, fear and self-condemnation? Have you experienced His Father-love and His forgiveness of all your unbelief and wrong attitudes? Have you received His peace, and freedom to be the person God created you to be? I trust that as you acted on the teaching and truths of the previous section of this book, you can say a definite YES to these questions. I realize it wasn't easy to let those chains go that had become a part of who you were. I know that sticky clay really wanted to pull you down, and resisted every effort to set you free, and perhaps even now some of it still clings to your feet, as you work to wash away every vestige of its memory. And now you sit there on that rock where God has placed you – free, enjoying the light of His face, but probably unsure of what happens now! Perhaps you feel like a wounded soldier, still reeling from the intensity of the battle and suffering from the hurts inflicted by the enemy over the past years of your imprisonment in his camp. These hurts might be physical, emotional or mental, and they are like continuous reminders of the past, and opportunities for the enemy to again accuse you. Maybe you're afraid of slipping off the rock, back into that pit of despair. All you want is to rest, to sleep, to be healed of those wounds and scars, to be strong again, to know the shalom of complete and total wholeness that God wants for you. Take heart, weary one! The Bible is replete with God's promises to restore and renew, especially in the lives of His children. Be encouraged as we look at some of these truths, and allow them to bring you His peace and hope. As you spend time in His presence, ask Him for the healing He has promised, and thank Him for it, even before there is manifest evidence of it!

God is indeed the <u>God of Restoration</u>. After David's sin with Bathsheba, and against Uriah, he asked God to restore the <u>joy</u> of His salvation, so he would then be able to show other sinners the way to Him (Psa.51:12-13). God wants to restore your joy (John 15:11; Rom.15:13; Isa.61:3). This is part of the package of His salvation (John 15:11; Rom.15:13). Receive it today with thanksgiving! And while you're rejoicing, claim the promise of Jer.30:17, where God says "I will restore <u>health</u> to you and <u>heal you of your wounds</u>", and in Psa.103:3 tells us the Lord… "<u>heals all your diseases</u>". With 3 John 2 "I pray that you may prosper in all things and be in health, just as your soul prospers"! He is the One who restores <u>your soul</u> from the wounds of the enemy, as you feed in the green pastures of His Word, and drink of the still waters of His peace (Psa.23:2-3). In Job 33:26, we read that "He restores to man <u>His righteousness</u>". You no longer need to be filled with guilt or shame, because He sees you clothed in His own righteousness, unspotted and pure. Know this and receive it as yours today!

In metaphorical language, God promises His people in Joel 2:25, 26 "I will restore to you <u>the years</u> that the locust has eaten ... You shall eat in plenty and be satisfied". You may be looking at your life right now with regrets for all the wasted years, those decades you wandered in the desert of doubt and unbelief, in defeat and depression, when you could have been doing exploits for God in the Land of Blessing. Instead of condemning yourself and looking back, (which is what Satan wants you to do), take Paul's words in Phil.3:13-14 as yours: "forgetting those things which are behind and reaching forward to those things which are ahead, I press toward the goal for the prize of the upward call of God in Christ Jesus." When God defeats the enemy in your life, He takes back from him everything he stole from you, and restores it to you (Luke 11:21-22), not as the damaged and desolate years they were, but restored to be fruitful and full of blessing. We read in Zech.9:11-12 that He "will restore double to you" who have been freed from the pit. Believe His words of hope and let Him restore the years of loss with years of prosperity, and the years of curses with double the years of blessing.

A word similar to 'restoration', which is a favorite with God, is the word 'renewal'. In the previous section of this book we dealt with the renewal of the mind (Rom.12:2; Eph.4:23), and will touch on it again here, because it is an ongoing process as we resume the walk of faith, away from the past and into the future with Christ, who has restored our soul. One reason we need to be restored and renewed is so that we are not tempted to return to the land of bondage from which we have been delivered. Tit.3:5 indicates that it is the work of the Holy Spirit to renew (transform) the life of a believer in every aspect, even in knowledge (Rom.8:11; 1 Pet.3:18; Acts 1:8; 2 Cor.4:16; Col.3:10). Be reminded that He will not do this without our co-operation and willingness - to put off the old thoughts, beliefs and deeds, and put on the new (Col.3:8-16; Eph.4:22-24). This, as we have seen, is the pro-

71

cess of sanctification, in which our responsibility is to repent of our participation in sins (past, present or generational) which has given access to the enemy into our soul, in the form of spirits of fear, lust, bitterness, etc. The Holy Spirit points these things out to us in order that we can repent of them, renounce them and cast them out. He is also part of the renewal process, as He opens the truth of the Word to us, to form new pathways of truth in our mind, replacing the old pathways of lies. Again our part in the mind-renewal is to actually read, study and meditate on the Word, so its truth becomes the mind of Christ in us.

In the Old Testament we find promises of God to renew specific qualities in us that may have flagged or diminished. In Isa.40:31 we are told that "those who wait (with hope) on the LORD shall renew their strength" so they can run and walk, and soar like eagles. In Psa.51:10 David prayed for the renewal of a steadfast spirit within him. I especially like Psa.103:5 that says "your youth is renewed"! When we have been wounded it takes time to regain strength, healing and restoration. Spend time with God in prayer and feeding on His Word, claiming the renewal He has promised. Rest in His unfailing, unconditional love, knowing that His Father heart rejoices over you with singing! (Zeph.3:17) Ask the Holy Spirit to fill you, guide you and teach you. Practice Phil.4:8 for daily therapy! Right now is a time for resting from the battle, for healing of the wounds, for restoration and renewal in the soul and spirit. Fill your house and your life with praise and worship songs, to keep you fixed on God. "Don't remind God how big your problems are; tell your problems how big your God is!" And exercise your authority in the name of Jesus to cast out any thought that is not of God! Let SHALOM reign!!

15

THE ROCK YOU STAND ON

Descriptions / synonyms for 'rock' include
dependable, fortress, support, anchor, cornerstone.

*T*he first part of God's rescue plan is lifting you out
of the horrible pit and miry clay. The next is placing
your feet on a rock. As your strength is renewed, and your
wounds are healed, you stand up and test your feet. Are they
steady? Are you ready to stand? What about the rock? Let's
examine this rock beneath your feet. Is the rock secure? Will
it support me? Yes, indeed! If God has placed you on a rock,
you can know without any doubt, that it is a safe place to
stand. As we look at the references to 'rock' in scripture we
will see that a rock is often used as a metaphor to describe
an attribute of God, or as an allegory of God Himself. We
find this particularly in the Psalms, but if we go back to the
Song of Moses, in Deuteronomy 32, it is cited several times
as well. In vs.3-4, Moses sings "Ascribe greatness to our
God. He is the Rock, His work is perfect; for all His ways
are justice, a God of truth, and without injustice; righteous
and upright is He." All of these adjectives describing God
show us that He is <u>dependable</u> - a Rock that won't let us
down or fail us. Sometimes, it is only after we have tried

any number of other support systems, or belief systems, or ways of living, that, like the children of Israel, we remember God is our Rock (Psa.78:35), and we realize we need to depend only on Him. We can cry out to God, our rock and fortress, to deliver, save, lead and guide us (Psa.31:2-3). As the Psalmist prays in Psa.71:6 "cause me to escape... save me...be my strong refuge to which I may resort continually ... for You are my Rock and my <u>fortress</u>." (Also see Psa.18:2-3). Have you ever been in a desperate situation, and bombarded by overwhelming circumstances that threatened your very life, or at least your sanity, so that you wanted more than anything to escape to some place safe? You're probably thinking, "More often than I can count!" If it's any consolation, you are not the only one! What is of real comfort is that we *do* have a place of refuge – in God, our fortress. A fortress is like a walled castle, to which you don't just flee for safety, but where you can *live* safely, all the time. God is the Rock that provides refuge for us, as expressed in Psa.94:22: "The LORD has been my defense, and my God the Rock of my refuge." Isaiah refers to Him as "the Rock of your stronghold" (Isa.17:10). You can be an inhabitant of this fortress. Prov.29:25 says "Whoever trusts in the LORD shall be safe". David wrote "You have been a shelter for me, a strong tower from the enemy." (Psa.61:3), and "You shall hide them ('those who trust in You') in the secret place of Your presence from the plots of man" (Psa.31:19-20).

Jesus taught a parable about a wise man who built his house on a rock. (Matt.7:24-25) He said that this wise man was like a person who hears Jesus' sayings, and does them. The Rock that is the <u>support</u> against the fierce storms and floods in our life is the Word of God, keeping us firm and unshakable. It is as we hear and obey the Word that it is implanted in our hearts and protects our lives from danger and destruction (Jas.1:21-25). See Josh.1:8 and Psa.1:1-3. How vital is the Word in our Lives! Let us choose to sit at Jesus' feet and hear His word (Luke 10:38-42). Let it renew our minds and cleanse our hearts (Eph.5:25b-26).

In Deut.32:15, reference is made to "the Rock of (our) salvation". Also see 2 Sam.22:47 and Psa.89:26. Psa.95:1 suggests that we "shout joyfully to the Rock of our Salvation". Here the word 'Rock' gives the sense of stability, and immovability. It reminds me of Heb.6:18-19, which describes the firm and unshakable "*hope* we have as <u>an anchor</u> of the soul". What is this hope that anchors our souls? According to Col.1:27 and 1 Tim.1:1 it is none other than Jesus Christ himself. He, who abides in us by His Spirit, is the 'hope of glory'. His Spirit in us is the guarantee that we are His, and we cannot be moved from this anchor of hope. (Eph.1:13-14). Jesus, Son of God and Son of Man, through His substitutionary death on the cross, becomes the Rock of *our* salvation as soon as we are born into the family of God. (Rom.8:15-16). What a steadfast Rock we have as an anchor!

Prophecies in Psa.118:22, "The stone which the builders rejected has become the chief <u>cornerstone</u>", and in Isa.28:16, "I lay in Zion a stone for a foundation, a tried stone, a precious cornerstone, a sure foundation", were fulfilled centuries later. Jesus quoted from Psa. 118:22 in reference to Himself. (Matt.21:42; Mark 12:10; Luke 20:17) Peter quoted it in Acts 4:10-12, and again in 1 Pet.2:4-8, proclaiming its fulfillment by Jesus Christ; He also quotes Isaiah's prophecy, adding that *we* are living stones, built up a spiritual house, on this foundational cornerstone. Paul elaborates on this in Eph.2:19-22, showing that *both Jews and Gentiles* "are being built together for a dwelling place of God in the Spirit … Jesus Christ Himself being the chief cornerstone". Yet, Jesus, the cornerstone so precious to us who believe, is a "stumbling stone and rock of offence" to those disobedient to the Word (Rom.9:33 and 1 Pet.2:8, quoting from Isa.8:14). If we stumble on a rock, and any part of us connects suddenly with it, we are hurt (offended by it). What was meant to be our refuge and salvation becomes our enemy. If we do not receive Jesus as our Savior, we must face Him as our judge (John 3:18-19, 36).

Here are some interesting *rock* facts from scripture for you to ponder ... When Moses asked to see God's glory, God said "stand on the rock while my glory passes by. I will put you in the cleft of the rock and will cover you with my hand while I pass by" (Exod.33:18-23) ... In reference to the journey of the Israelites from Egypt to Canaan, 1 Cor. 10:4 tells us that they "all drank of that spiritual Rock that followed them, and that Rock was Christ" ... Hanna, in praise to God when He heard her prayer for a child, said "nor is there any rock like our God" (1 Sam.2:2) ... Isaiah prophesied about the coming King in Isa.32:2, describing Him "as the shadow of a great rock in a weary land" ... King David, so familiar with the Rock of his salvation, his refuge and his stronghold, said at the end of his life "The Rock of Israel *spoke* to me" (2 Sam.23:3-4) ... In Moses' last speech to Israel, he said they were unmindful of the Rock who *begot* them, and had forgotten the God who fathered them (Deut.32:18). About the heathen nations around them he said "*their* rock is not like *our* Rock" (Deut.32:31) ... In the end many who despise God the Rock, will call on the rocks to hide them from God's wrath! (Rev.6:15-16)

"Who is a rock, except our God?" (Psa.18:31) "He is *my* rock" (Psa.92:15). "The LORD is my rock and my fortress and my deliverer, the God of my strength, in whom I will trust" (2 Sam.22:2-3). "Lead me to the rock that is higher than I" (Psa.61:2). "The LORD lives! Blessed be my Rock! Let the God of my salvation be exalted" (Psa.18:46). You can trust the Rock where He has placed your feet! AMEN!

16

"STANDING" ORDERS

*A*mong human-kind, the process of growth and development from birth to approximately a year old is fairly consistent and quite predictable. Apart from differences in the length of time between each notable stage, we know that a baby usually learns to roll over before he can sit up. Most babies can crawl before they can walk, though not all always crawl! But I think we can say for certain that before you or I were able to walk, we learned to stand (not just pulling ourselves up to a standing position beside a chair, but standing alone, unsupported, and steady). As soon as we accomplished this feat, the whole household made it their duty to see that we got those feet of ours moving in a beeline from one pair of hands to another away over there! What was the rush? How many times did we fall before we mastered the art of walking? Maybe we should have practiced standing more, so we would be steadier on our walking feet! The same principles apply to someone who has been in an accident, or had a crippling disease – learning to walk again takes time. Rushing into walking before learning to stand can cause embarrassing falls, and feelings of discouragement. In our spiritual life, we cannot be lifted out of the pit of miry clay, and immediately know how to walk with God.

We need to learn to stand *before* Him, *with* Him and *in* Him, until our feet are steady and strong.

In what is deemed to be the first book of scripture to be written, Elihu admonished Job to "Stand still and consider the wondrous works of God." (Job 37:14) Job had sort of been wallowing in self-pity in the midst of his physical suffering, and anguish over the loss of his family. He was tending to blame God for his situation, and wishing he'd never been born. He didn't understand that his troubles were by Satan's design (Job 1 and 2). As time passed with no relief, Job seemed to lose sight of the God he had loved and served for many years. Before all this started, it seemed that he was filled with fear (Job 1:5), and as is usually the case, his fears were fulfilled (Job 3:25). Later, more fears surfaced (Job 9:28; 30:15). As we read through his responses to his 'comforters', we also detect an unhealthy dose of self-righteousness. In his preoccupation with himself, he needed to refocus his vision back to God, to stand before Him and meditate on Him and His wonderful deeds. As soon as Elihu finished speaking, God came to Job with a revelation of His might, wisdom and holiness (Job 38:1-40:2), and Job had no answer. Then God challenged Job's self pre-occupation (Job 40:6-41:34), and Job responded with deep repentance, which resulted in restoration (ch.42).

We, too, need to learn to stand before God in order to:

1. behold His glory and contemplate His amazing works (Psa.8);
2. hear Him speak His will to us (1 Kings 17:1-4; Ezek.2:1-2);
3. renew our covenant with Him (Deut.29:10-13);
4. minister in His name (Deut.18:5; 10:8);

5. receive a miracle (Exod. 14:13; Josh.3:17; 1 Sam.12:16);
6. pray and give praise to God (2 Chron.20:3-12; Psa.134:1-2);
7. confess our sins and worship the Lord (Neh.9:2-3);
8. have victory over the powers of darkness (Eph.6:10-18).

Find the secret to standing in Psa. 20. Especially note vs.7-8. We have risen and stand upright because we trust in the Lord!

At the beginning of the second chapter of Ephesians, Paul wrote about how we were dead in trespasses and sins, living under Satan's rule, doing whatever felt good to our fleshly mind, and ultimately under God's judgment. Verse 4 opens with the words "But God, who is rich in mercy, because of His great love with which He loved us..." When God steps into our lives, miracles begin. In the next two verses, in just a few words, Paul relates what God actually did for us because of His mercy and His great love for us. These precious truths show us how we actually <u>stand with Christ</u> – now! It's really impossible for our human minds to understand the magnitude of what God has done for us, and where He has placed us. Maybe the most amazing part is that we didn't do a thing to deserve any of it, nor can we ever repay Him for all He's done. While we were spiritually dead in our sins and trespasses, separated from God, He:

- "made us alive *together* with Christ" (Col.2:13)
- "raised us up *together*" (Col.2:12; Col.3:1).
- "made us sit *together* in the heavenly places" (Col.3:3)

Notice the repetition of the words "together with". Our Father wants us to be with His Son, and in His mind we are in heaven with Him right now. And Jesus wants to be with us while we're still in our bodies, so He sent His Spirit, who lives in us. Through Christ's death we are actually in God's throne room of grace by His Spirit (Rom.5:1-2; Eph.2:18; 3:12; Heb.4:14-16). As we learn to spend time with Christ, we will find we will continuously walk in sweet fellowship with Him in the Spirit. This delights God's heart, and He will become the delight of our heart as well.

The Apostle Paul, facing possible death in a Roman prison, writes in Philippians chapter three about his resurrection hope and pressing onward in the call of God. Then, he exhorts the believers at Philippi "Therefore... stand fast in the Lord" (Phil.4:1). He had found the key to a joy that sustained him through horrendous trials and persecution (2 Cor.11:23-27). It was 'knowing Christ' and being "found in Him" (Phil.3:7-10). Nothing else mattered. In his letter to the Ephesian church he wrote that God *chose us in Christ*, to *bless us in Christ;* and *we are accepted in Christ* because *we trusted in Christ.* (Study the entire panoramic word-picture of our standing in Christ in Eph.1:3-23). Paul continues in Eph.2:6: *God sees us in Christ, where Christ is – in heaven!* And in v.7, *because we are in Christ, we receive God's lavish grace and kindness.* V.10 – *God created us in Christ to walk in good works which He will complete in us* (Phil.1:6).

Dear friend, do you comprehend, at least to some extent, what it means to stand in Christ? Think about it – when God looks at you He sees His perfect, sinless Son, because you are hidden in Him (Col.3:3). He already sees you there in heaven with Him, as pure as He is. He raised us with His Son to be citizens of heaven (Phil.3:20). Let us stand in the Lord, living as children of Light and citizens of heaven. "Seek those things which are above...Set your mind on things above, not on things on the earth" (Col.3:1-4). The fact is, we are still in our earthly bodies, with freedom to choose to live for God, or not (Col.3:5-17). If we say we know and love God, and yet live a life contrary to His will, driven by our fleshly desires, we are lying, and the truth is not in us (1 John 1:3-6). We must remember who we are in Christ, and that we are empowered by the Holy Spirit and the Word to live a life pleasing to Him, so we stand unashamed at His coming (1 John 2:28-29).

17

STANDING IN THE FAITH

S truck down on the Damascus Road by a blinding light, Saul of Tarsus, number one antagonist of his time to the Way, (Acts 9:1-2) was transformed by the grace of God into the Apostle Paul, expounder and proponent of this Way. By special revelation from God for a period of several years, God opened up to him the truths of the Way, which he called the Gospel (good news), and confirmed His calling on Paul's life to proclaim this Gospel (Rom.1:1), in particular to the Gentiles (non-Jews) (Eph.3:1-12). Preaching the Gospel and defending the Gospel became Paul's life-long passion. Under the direction of the Holy Spirit he travelled and preached the Gospel, establishing churches in cities all across the area to the north of Jerusalem and the Mediterranean Sea, into Syria, Galatia, Asia, Greece, Rome etc. It was his concern that the new believers be grounded in the Gospel truth, which he referred to as 'The Faith'. He soon learned that false teachers (no doubt by special assignment of our enemy, Satan) would come and try to draw the believers away from the Gospel of grace, into heresy or apostasy. If news of this happening reached Paul's ears, he would send someone to set them straight, or write a letter to the church, to warn against these 'false gospels', and "contend for the faith" (Jude 3).

In all of Paul's letters in the scripture canon, from Romans to Titus, he faithfully presents a record of the basic tenets of the faith, confident of what God had revealed to him, and faithful in expounding it. But in his letters to the Galatians and Timothy, as well the Colossians, he also finds it necessary to vehemently "defend and confirm the Gospel" (Phil.1:7). In writing to the young pastor, Timothy, he warned against the teaching of any other doctrine, and said that some had strayed from the faith (1 Tim.1:3-11). He charged Timothy to "wage the good warfare, having faith and a good con-science, which some having rejected, concerning the faith have suffered shipwreck" (1 Tim.1:18-19). In 1 Tim.4, Paul warns about apostasy, and departure from the faith (v.1), and admonishes Timothy in v.6 "If you instruct the brethren in these things, you will be a good minister of Jesus Christ, nourished in the words of faith and of the good doctrine which you have carefully followed." A concerned exhorta-tion follows in 1 Tim.6:12 to "Fight the good fight of faith, lay hold on eternal life to which you were also called and have confessed the good confession in the presence of many witnesses." Finally in ch.6:20-21, hear the pathos in his words, "O Timothy! Guard what was committed to your trust, avoiding the profane and idle babblings and contradic-tions of what is falsely called knowledge - by professing it some have strayed concerning the faith."

Later, Paul sent Timothy another letter about keeping the faith, with the following warnings:

- 2 Tim.1:13-14 – "Hold fast the pattern of sound words which you have heard from me, in faith and love which are in Christ Jesus. That good thing which was committed to you, *keep by the Holy Spirit* who dwells in us."

- 2 Tim.2:1-2 – "Be strong in the grace that is in Christ Jesus. And the many things that you have heard from me ... *commit these to faithful men who will be able to teach others also.*"
- 2 Tim.3:14 – "You must *continue in the things which you have learned and been assured of.*
- 2 Tim.4:2-5 - "Preach the word! Be ready in season and out of season. Convince, rebuke, exhort, with all longsuffering and teaching. The time will come when they will not endure sound doctrine, but according to their own desires, because they have itching ears, they will heap up for themselves teachers; and they will turn their ears away from the truth... But you *be watchful in all things* ... do the work of an evangelist; *fulfill your ministry.*"

Near the end of this letter Paul testifies "I have fought the good fight, I have finished the race; *I have kept the faith.*" Yes, indeed! He preached the faith, kept the faith and contended for the faith.

I encourage you to study the book of Galatians, in which Paul defends his apostleship, and the Gospel of grace he preached, in the face of Judaizers who were bringing in teachings of works and of keeping the law, thus nullifying the Gospel of grace. I quote some of his words: "O foolish Galatians! Who has bewitched you that you should not obey the truth? Did you receive the Spirit by the works of the law or by the hearing of faith? Are you so foolish? Having begun in the Spirit, are you now being made perfect by the flesh?" (Gal.3:1-3) "You are no longer a slave, but a son ... an heir of God" (Gal.4:7). "Stand fast ... in the liberty by which Christ has made us free, and do not be entangled again with a yoke of bondage" (Gal.5:1). A 'faith' based on our efforts is not faith at all. It is dead works! How important it is to stand firm in the faith, so we will not falter when trials or false teachers or the enemy's lies assail us. (See Col.2:6-23).

There are references to the importance of standing in the faith and being established in it, in Paul's other letters as well i.e. Rom.5:2 – "We have access by faith into *this grace in which we stand*, and rejoice in hope." In 1 Cor. 2:5 Paul says our faith should not be in the wisdom of men, but *in the power of God*. In 1 Cor.15:1 reference is made to standing *in the Gospel which Paul preached*. Phil.1:27 tells us as believers to *"stand fast in one spirit*, with one mind striving together for *the faith of the Gospel*. (At the beginning of this verse Paul says, "Only let your conduct be worthy of the Gospel of Christ". Is it??) Col.4:12 says we are to "stand perfect and complete in *all the will of God* (i.e. *the faith*). 1 Thes.3:2 – Timothy was sent to the church in Thessalonica to establish them concerning their faith. Paul wanted them to "be pre-served blameless at the coming of our Lord Jesus Christ" (1 Thes.5:23). The book of Hebrews talks about coming to God "in full assurance of faith", and "holding fast the confes-sion of our hope without wavering, for He who promised is faithful … looking unto Jesus, the author and finisher of our faith" (Heb.10:23; 12:2).

2 Cor.13:5 tells us to examine ourselves to see if we are really in the faith. Do we simply have head-knowledge of the truth of the Gospel, or have we experienced the changing power of His grace in our hearts by confessing Him as our Savior from sin, with a belief that takes us in to a life of right living (Rom.10:8-10). Does your faith measure up against the yardstick found in 1 Pet.1? Will your faith stand firm in the storms of adversity, temptation, or persecution? "Build yourselves up on your most holy faith, (by) praying in the Holy Spirit" (Jude 20).

18

STANDING IN THE BATTLE

ou're probably thinking, "It's not a good idea to *stand* in the middle of a battle, unless you have a death wish", and that's correct. But the battle we'll talk about today is *different* in several respects. It's a spiritual battle. This means we are not physically 'up in arms' against other human beings, or any visible enemy. Our fight is a real one, and a constant one, but it is against "principalities, against powers, against the rulers of the darkness of this age, against spiritual hosts of wickedness in the heavenly places" (Eph.6:12). Yes, when Satan was cast out of heaven, he set up a hierarchy of these wicked fallen angels (demons) in the second heaven, a kingdom of extreme evil, with the express purpose of defeating the works of God in and through His people. But, you say, "Wasn't Satan defeated at the cross, when Jesus (the seed of the woman) bruised his head?" (Gen.3:15) Yes, and apparently the blow to his head enraged him (Rev.12:17). Because he has been defeated, we have the power to overcome him through the blood of the Lamb and our confession of faith in Jesus. (Rev.12:11). Satan is a deceiver, a liar and a blackmailer, and still defeats people through accusation (Rev.12:10) and guilt, unless we are onto his tactics, and call his bluff, by not accepting his endless lies, and accusations, and by reminding him that we have been forgiven. Not only that, Jesus has given us authority over Satan, through His Name. (Mark 16:17-18; Luke 10:17-19). You, as a Spirit-filled believer have this authority. We are not told to pray for God to resist and rebuke the devil, but we ourselves are to cast him from us in Jesus' powerful name.

That there is a battle and that we are called to this battle is evident throughout the scriptures. The stories of actual physical battles in the Old Testament, usually between God's chosen people, and the wicked nations they were to conquer, are pictures of the spiritual battles we are engaged in as God's church today. Often it seems that we, too, are fighting in one sense against people, not realizing that then, as now, Satan uses people to sling his arrows at us, but our enemy is not the person he uses, but Satan himself. We need to take a stand against the enemy, but it is God Who fights the battle and wins the victory (Deut.1:30). i.e. When the Israelites were in slavery in Egypt, God called Moses to go and bring them out of Egypt, and into the place He had promised to them (Exod.3:2-22). He told Moses to 'stand before Pharaoh' (Exod.8:20; 9:13) and speak the word of the LORD to Him. From that point on, until the Israelites were free, and Pharaoh's army was decimated (Exod.4:29 - 14:31), Moses just obeyed; he stood and watched God fight against Pharaoh (really, the enemy was Satan, not Pharaoh). Moses did not physically fight. He used the words God put in his mouth, and the rod in his hand to demonstrate the might and power of God over the enemy and over the idols of Egypt. Deliverance came through obedience and dependence on God. In Exod.14:13-16, Moses said to the people "Stand still, and see the salvation of the LORD ... The LORD will fight for you". That's exactly what happened! Later, when they faced Amalek, Moses stood before God on the top of a hill with the rod of God in his hand, battling in prayer for the victory (Eph.6:18), his tiring hands held up by Aaron and Hur. (Exod.17:8-13) ... Esther went to battle on behalf of her people, when she fasted in prayer for three days, then went in and stood before the king, at risk to her life, to plead for them; and the king gave them authority to fight back against those who had received orders to kill them. (Our King, also, has given us authority to resist and fight our enemy!) ... King Jehoshaphat said to his frightened army, "Do not be afraid ... The battle is not yours but God's ... Position yourselves, stand still and see the salvation of the Lord, who is with you" (2 Chron.20:15-17). Jehoshaphat fought the battle of prayer and praise (vs.5-12). (Read about it in vs.18-30!) ... Later, God chided the prophets of Israel for their failure to "stand in battle for the house of Israel" (Ezek.13:5)

We have seen that one secret to victory is to know that the battle is not ours, but God's; it's always been His. When we try to conquer evil in our own strength, we become even more defeated. Be encouraged by Psa.18:32, 34-35, 39! Another secret to victory is to know the enemy. In Eph.6:11, 13, Paul says we are to stand against the *wiles* (schemes, tricks) of the devil. But before he tells us how to stand, or how to defeat him, he tells us in verse 12 what we are up against. We're not just shadow-boxing – this is real! Seriously! Satan himself has hoodwinked many into believing either that he doesn't exist or pose a problem for us, or that if we ignore him he'll go away. The Bible doesn't teach this. We are told to be vigilant and resist the devil (Jas.4:7; 1 Pet.5:8-9). (Also see Acts 5:3; 2 Cor.11:13-15; Eph.4:27; 1 Tim.3:7; 2 Tim.2:26). God has provided us with weapons and defenses against Satan (Refer back to chapter 13 on Anti-Virus Protection). Our orders are to stand in the battle against him in the authority of Christ, claiming the victory over him that was won at the cross (1 Cor.15:57). Even a standing soldier resists the onslaught by using his shield to deflect the weapons of the enemy (Eph.6:16). Satan will attack us with his lies, and with wounding arrows, unless we stand against Him with the truth and by the power of Jesus' name.

In 1 Tim.1:18-19 Paul charged Timothy to "wage the good warfare, having faith and a good conscience", and in ch.6:12 to "Fight the good fight of faith". In 2 Tim. 2:3-4, he adds a warning to the business of being "a good soldier of Jesus Christ". First he said he must endure hardship, and second, that "No one engaged in warfare entangles himself with the affairs of this life, that he may please Him who enlisted him as a soldier". This reminds me of Heb.12:1, "Let us lay aside every weight, and the sin which so easily ensnares us" (i.e. Col.3:8). Remember the resounding defeat Joshua and his army experienced at Ai? (Josh.7) One reason for the defeat was presuming victory and proceeding without God's direction. But when Joshua fell on his face before God to ask why He had let them down, God rebuked him, saying that there was sin in the camp. He told him to tell Israel "You cannot stand before your enemies until you take away the accursed thing from among you" (vs.10-13). See also Judg.2:11-14. Victory over Satan is ours, but sin in our lives, no matter how we rationalize and excuse it, will give Satan the victory over us. This is not God's will. James tells us to resist the devil, and draw near to God, then adds, "Cleanse your hands, you sinners, and purify your hearts, you double minded" (Jas,4:7-8). In other words, in order to have victory over the world, the flesh and the devil, we need to turn to God in repentance, renounce the sin(s) and receive forgiveness, so we may be lifted up (v.9-10). This gives us the ability to stand in the battle, victorious over the enemy in the power of Christ (1 Cor.15:57).

19

FEET MADE FOR WALKING
🌺

*P*lease read Psalm 25, written by David - a plea for deliverance (vs.2, 19-20), forgiveness (6-11, 18) and guidance (4-5, 12). In anticipation of an answer, he writes "My eyes are ever toward the LORD, for *He shall pluck my feet out of the net*" (v.15). This is where the victory-walk starts for the child of God. It is as we repent, and receive forgiveness of sin, that deliverance comes from God, the only One who can extricate us from the net that has ensnared us. He then *places our feet on a rock,* suggesting security (Psa.40:2); *in a wide place*, inferring freedom (Psa.31:8); and *before God's face*, implying companionship (Psa.41:12). He also *protects our feet from harm* (1 Sam.2:9; Psa.121:3; Psa.66:9; Psa.18:36). Just as our physical feet can slip or trip at times, or take us into dangerous places, so it is with our spiritual feet – the feet that are made for walking with God may slip and cause us to lose ground; they may stumble, and throw us head first into the 'slough of despond', or the sinking sand of doubt and fear. They may wander off the narrow path (Matt.7:14), and get tangled up in the snares of the enemy. Rather than pretending we are coping with these situations, or threshing about and only making it worse, may we remember David's prayer in Psalm 25, remember that our hope is in the LORD, and that deliverance comes from Him, as we are willing to let Him pick us up, clean us off, and set our feet back into His way. Like a child who has stumbled, call out for help from our dear, caring Father! What is the secret to receiving His protection? Stay close to Him, keep your hand in His, and listen to His words.

Feet that walk in God's ways must be feet that are *cleansed*, just as the priests washed their feet before entering the tabernacle or offering sacrifices to the LORD (Exod.30:19-21). It was a sign of sanctification, getting rid of the dust and grime of the world that clings to us so readily, and demonic parasites that steal and destroy if not washed off (1 Cor.6:11; Tit.3:5; Eph.5:25b-26). When the priests were ordained, the blood of a ram was applied to the big toe of their right foot (Exod.29:20; Lev.14:14), to show that they were *consecrated* to walk in righteous paths. This is a picture of the blood of Jesus, the spotless Lamb of God cleansing our conscience from dead works to serve the living God – from following self-righteousness to walking in Christ's righteousness (Heb.9:11-14). After the sprinkling with blood the same toe was anointed with oil (Lev.14:15-18). This symbolized being *commissioned*, given the power and authority of an office. The New Testament fulfillment of this is cited in Acts 10:38: "God anointed Jesus of Nazareth with the Holy Spirit and with power, who went about doing good and healing all who were oppressed by the devil, for God was with Him." Saul of Tarsus was in turn commissioned by Jesus to take the Gospel message of forgiveness, deliverance and sanctification to the Gentiles (Acts26:16-18). Have we been commissioned? YES! "You shall receive power when the Holy Spirit has come upon you, and you shall be witnesses to me … to the end of the earth" – Jesus' words to His church in Acts 1:8. (Also see Mark 16:15-18). This is referred to in Eph.6:15, as our feet being "shod with the preparation (or readiness) of the Gospel of peace". Are your feet prepared (cleansed, consecrated and commissioned) to take the Gospel of peace to the world?

How many times have you looked at a pair of feet and thought how beautiful they were? (other than baby's feet of course). On the whole, most feet, especially if they've been around the block a few times, are not that pretty. Think about it – what's that attractive about corns, bunions and plantar warts? What about the cracked skin and calluses, the hammer toes, toenail fungus and ingrown toenails? Then there are flat feet and club feet, fallen arches and bone spurs. Some people have diseased feet or broken feet. When you realize everything our feet have been through (literally), it's a wonder any of us is still able to stand, let alone walk. God gave us a pretty solid under-standing and maybe words like tough and durable might well describe our feet. But, some feet are special in God's eyes. Through the prophet Isaiah He says, "How *beautiful* upon the mountains are the feet of him who brings good news, who proclaims peace, who brings glad tidings of good things, who proclaims salvation, who says to Zion, 'Your God reigns'." (Isa.52:7) Paul quotes from this passage in Rom.10:15, in reference to those who preach the Gospel. I would venture to say that the feet of those who carry and proclaim the Good News of Salvation through Jesus Christ are beautiful to God not only on the mountains, but wherever they are found. My ugly feet would not matter a whit to me, if they are beautiful to God. May we run with the Good-News feet of Eph.6:15, letting our 'beautiful' feet bless others!

In the culture of the Old Testament day, when battles were fought with hand weapons, and victory was decided by who was fleeing and who was pursuing, the winners would proclaim victory by placing their foot on the neck of their conquered foe (Josh.10:24). This is possibly referenced in Psa.110:1: "The LORD said unto my Lord, "Sit at my right hand, till I make Your enemies Your footstool." (Also see 2 Sam.22:38-41). So, when I read "You shall tread upon the lion and the cobra; the young lion and the serpent you shall trample underfoot", in Psa. 91:13, I sit up and take notice. I really believe the word 'lion' refers to none other than "our adversary the devil who walks about like a roaring lion, seeking whom he may devour" (1 Pet.5:8), and 'serpent' to "that serpent of old, called the Devil and Satan, who deceives the whole world" (Rev.12:9), the same one that "deceived Eve by his craftiness" (2 Cor.11:3). I doubt I will ever forget the excitement I felt a few months ago, when in my Bible reading for the day, as I was plowing through the names, greetings and admonitions of Romans 16, I found an incredible statement, which came to me as a special personal promise, in verse 20: "And the God of peace will crush Satan under your feet shortly". It was a confirmation of Jesus' words in Luke 10:19; "Behold, I give you the authority to trample on serpents and scorpions, and over all the power of the enemy, and nothing shall by any means hurt you." Amen! God has plans for our feet to be *vanquishing, and victorious,* in the powerful name of Jesus, and by the authority He gives us. Notice that Rom.16:20 does not say *we* will crush Satan – God does the crushing – but we have to *put* Satan under our feet if we want God to *crush* him under our feet! We are not to give any place to the devil except under our feet! (Eph.4:27) I have never *seen* a demon or an evil spirit, but many times over the past two years, I have encountered them, and cast them out in that Name above all names, which all the powers of evil must obey. They left, 'often kicking and screaming', definitely trampled on and vanquished. Are your feet ready for victory?

20

THE PATH HE PLANNED

𝓗 ow would you describe a path? There are a few words that apply to every path, but there are many different kinds of paths. Some are rocky, steep and dangerous; others are quiet, peaceful and idyllic. Some paths are twisting, narrow and hard to see; others are wide, straight and well lit. God has planned a path or way for each of His children. In some respects, we are all on the same path, because there is only one way (John 14:6). And yet we know that our journeys with God are as varied as we are. Usually our path becomes what we make it, a result of our choices, past and present. It is our choice whether we follow Him, in His way, or go our own way within His chosen way. We often go down rabbit trails, seeking some temporary diversion that leads us into trouble, and we learn that the way back to His way is not easy. Isaiah writes "Your ears shall hear a word behind you, saying, 'This is the way, walk in it'." (Isa.30:21) It is as we listen for His voice, and obey Him, that we realize that "*His way is perfect*" and "*He makes my way perfect*" (Psa.18:30, 32). Now that your feet are prepared and ready to walk, it is time to "Ponder the path of your feet, and let all your ways be established" (Prov.4:26). What are some signs that show us we are indeed on the right path? Watch for these <u>signposts</u> <u>along the way</u>:

- **Righteousness – Psa.23:3**   **- Love – Rom.5:5; 1 Jn.2:5**

- **Peace – Phil.4:6-9; Rom.5:1** **- Grace – Eph.2:5-8**

- **Light –John 8:12; 1 Pet.2:9** **- Life – John10:10; 14:6**

- **Wisdom – Col.1:9; 2:3; 3:16** **- Forgiveness – Col.1:14**

- **Joy – Psa.16:11; Rom.14:17** **- Holiness – Eph.1:4**

- **Hope –Col.1:27; 1 Pet.1:3**   **- Truth – Jn.16:13; Eph.4:15**

- **Freedom – Jn. 8:32, 36**   **- God's presence – Heb.13:5**

If right now you are thinking that you are not on a path of peace, joy, hope or forgiveness; if you can't find any of these signposts; if you are wandering aimlessly in the dark, call out to God as David did. If you seek Him with all your heart, you will find Him (Jer.29:11-13). Make sure today that you are one of His children, born again by the Holy Spirit into a new life in Christ – not on the basis of your good works, but because of Jesus' death on the cross, taking the penalty of your sin so you could have everlasting life. If you are indeed a child of God, but have listened to the lies of the enemy, and are living in defeat and despair, you, too, can experience restoration and renewal through His grace. Ask God to show you by His Spirit things in your life that have entangled you, and left you stuck in the miry clay at the bottom of a horrible pit. Repent of giving place to the devil, and receive God's forgiveness. Cast out the spirits of bitterness, fear, guilt, anger, accusation, etc. in the name of Jesus. Let your kind Shepherd release you from your chains, fill you with His

Spirit and teach you His word. Let His love enfold you, and restore your soul, placing you back on His path of holiness and light, to walk with Him and talk with Him along the way towards home! You will enjoy the journey with your fellow travelers if you have settled all your accounts, and are free to love them as brothers and sisters.

We've talked about God's perfect path, with signposts to show us the way. Let's look now at some of the ways the scriptures describe the path itself. David calls it "the path of life", full of joy in God's presence, and eternal pleasures at His right hand (Psa.16:11). If that was all we were told about this path, it should certainly be enough to give us a desire to find it and walk on it! In Psalm 65:11 David says "Your paths drip with abundance", reminding me of the beautiful words of 2 Pet.1:3-4 describing all the blessings and promises we have to enjoy along the path, and the inheritance we receive at the end of the road! Again, in Psa.25:10 David exclaims "*All* the paths of the LORD are mercy and truth." Where would we be apart from His mercy and His truth? Definitely not on the path of life! In Psa.27:11 David asks the LORD to lead him in a plain (straight) path, and maybe later realized what this would be, when he prayed, "Make me walk in the path of Your commandments, for I delight in it" (Psa.119:35). Of course, the book of Proverbs has some insight into the paths of God as well. In Prov.10:29 we are told that "The way of the LORD is strength for the upright". Perhaps it's like the path beside the still waters, and through the green pastures where our soul is restored as the Good Shepherd leads us in the paths of righteousness (Psa.23). Prov.15:19 comments that the way of the upright is a highway, and in 16:17, that the highway of the upright is to depart from evil. (I assume that's the *high* way as opposed to the *low* way!) In His Sermon on the Mount Jesus described the way which leads to life as narrow or difficult (Matt.7:14), a way that very few find (sad but true). Near the end of His earthly ministry, He told His disciples that He Himself was the Way. Hebrews explains this in ch.10:19-20: The blood of Jesus made it possible for us to enter the Holy of Holies, into the very presence of God, by a new and living way, Jesus Himself, whose body, like the veil, was torn for us, giving us access to the throne of grace, to find grace and mercy from the Father (Heb.4:14-16).

As our 'heavenly travel agent', God has our trip with Him planned from start to finish, all laid out in His mind before time began. What a relief that we don't have to fret over the details, or worry if we'll make the connections, "for the LORD knows the way of the righteous" (Psa.1:6; 142:3). So, relax, and enjoy the trip – you're in good hands. In fact, He encompasses our path, and is acquainted with all our ways (Psa.139:3, KJV). We can be assured that His wisdom will lead us in right paths, so when we walk our steps will not be hindered, and when we run, we will not stumble (Prov.4:11-12). He has made sure of this by providing His word as a lamp to our feet and a light to our path (Psa.119:105). SO, in order to keep to the path He has laid out for us, we need to leave the driving to Him, not trying to take over the controls when the path gets bumpy, or when the enemy sends his lightning-bolt darts into our path – We are safe only as we stay in the way, and let our pilot and guide and protector do what only He knows how to do to keep us on a safe course. Oh, did I forget to tell you about the thieves and robbers lying in ambush along the path? Just another reason to walk close to the One who gives us ammunition and weapons to use against them!

"The Lord is my Shepherd; I shall not want. He makes me to lie down in green pastures; He leads me beside the still waters. He restores my soul; He leads me in the paths of

righteousness for His name's sake. You (my Shepherd) prepare a table before me in the presence of my enemies." Yes,
there are enemies nearby, but we are safe if we stay with the
Shepherd. We can walk His path in His peace! (Psa.23)

21

DIRECTED STEPS

"It is not in man who walks to direct his own steps"
Jeremiah 10:23

*O*ur feet are ready to walk, and the path has been prepared, so let's reach out, take the Father's hand, and
step out in faith into the greatest adventure ever, placing one
tentative foot ahead of the other, again and again. Gradually,
perhaps after a few falls, our steps become steady and sure.
As we breathe in the heavenly oxygen of the Holy Spirit,
and are refreshed by His water of life and the green pastures
of the Word, we are strengthened for the journey. One very
comforting thought for us to remember throughout this life
journey comes to us from Psa.85:13 – "Righteousness will
go before Him, and shall make *His footsteps our pathway."*
The same theme is echoed in 1 Pet.2:21. Just as a child walks
in the footsteps of his father, we are to walk in the steps of
Jesus, who has gone before, and who still goes before to show
us the way. It's a brand new path to us, and we don't know
what lies ahead. We can't really make plans for the journey
(Jer.10:23), but we can trust the One who goes before us, to
guide us, enable us and protect us.

Have you ever thought about the faith and trust it took for Abram to step out into the path God called him to take? The instructions weren't all that clear. In short, "Get out of your country, leave your family home, and your relatives, and start walking – as you go I'll lead you, and then I'll tell you when to stop. Apparently Abram was up for the adventure, even though he was already 75 years old! (Gen.12:1-5) We are told nothing about what must have been a long, arduous journey, just that he departed, and he arrived. I wonder if his faith ever wavered, and he questioned if God had really called him to this path. He must have learned of God's faithfulness to direct his steps, because of what he did later in life. His wife Sarah died when he was 137 years old, and after the funeral, as he watched his 37 year-old son, Isaac, mourning his mother's death, he knew it was time to find a wife for him. He dispatched his servant, Eliezer, to travel back to his home country to find the right bride for Isaac. (How would you like that responsibility?) Read the story in Gen.24. Please note what Abraham said to reassure Eliezer. (The LORD) "will send His angel before you" (v.7). When God actually led Eliezer directly to the home of beautiful Rebecca, he blessed God for His mercy and truth toward Abraham. Then he said, "As for me, <u>being on the way</u>, *the LORD led me…*" (v.27). It seems that if we want God to guide our steps, we need to be on His path.

God may lead us in a variety of ways. As with Eliezer, he sometimes sends angels to lead us. Angels directed the women at the empty tomb of Jesus to tell the disciples Jesus had risen, and would meet them in Galilee (Matt.28:5-7). Several stories of angel intervention and guidance are recorded in the book of Acts. There was deliverance from prison, and direction to preach in the temple (Acts5:19-21); Philip was directed by an angel to go to Gaza (Acts 8:26); an angel directed Cornelius to send for Peter in Joppa (Acts

10:3-5); and Peter was delivered from chains, and led out of prison by an angel (Acts 12:7-11).

Prior to the incarnation, *the Son of God appeared several times as The Angel of the LORD*/God. He met Hagar in her hour of need, and sent her back to Abram's house (Gen.16:7-13). He went before the Israelites, in a pillar of cloud and fire, after their deliverance from Egypt (Exod.14:19; Num.20:16); God promised that this same Angel would keep them in the way, and bring them into the place He had prepared for them (Exod.23:20). This is confirmed to have been fulfilled, in Isa.63:8-10. Gideon was guided by this Angel to defeat Israel's enemies (Judg.6:11-23); Elijah received direction several times from the Angel of the LORD (1 Kings 19:5-18; 2 Kings 1:2-4, 15).

I believe God still uses angels today, but we also have His Word and His Holy Spirit to guide us to an even greater measure than in the Old Testament. God told Moses in Exod.18:20 to teach the people His statues and laws and "show them the way in which they must walk". It was the Holy Spirit who directed Paul on his missionary journeys (Acts 16:7; 21:4). He also *guides our steps* in the way we should go, protecting us from harm, and giving us power to live as God's people in today's crazy world! Keep your heart tuned to hear His still, small voice!

God has the prerogative to lead us by whatever means He sees fit. One thing is certain – *He does lead us!* "*He will teach us His ways*, and we shall walk in His paths" (Isa.2:3; Mic.4:2). "I will instruct you and teach you in the way you should go; *I will guide you with My eye*" (Psa.32:8). "The steps of a good man are *ordered by the Lord* ... the Lord upholds him" (Psa.37:23-24). "A man's heart plans his way, but *the Lord directs his steps*" (Prov.16:9). "In all your

ways acknowledge Him, and *He shall direct your paths*"
(Prov.3:6). As this verse indicates, His guidance is available,
it's part of the package, but this isn't a forced march. Are you
ready and willing to let Him guide you on His path? "Show
me your ways, O LORD; teach me your paths. Lead me in
Your truth and teach me" (Psa.25:4-5). "Guide our feet into
the way of peace" (Luke 1:79). Also see Psa.17:5.

God not only *directs our steps* in His way, He *guards and
protects our steps*. The wisdom of His word leads us in
right paths, and as a result He promises, "When you walk,
your steps will not be hindered, and when you run you will
not stumble" (Prov.4:11-12). (It's not just about walking
– you're allowed to run too! – Just keep in touch with the
Guide). God provides His word to be a lamp to our feet, and
a light to our path, to show us any obstacles or dangers in
the way. In one of David's darkest moments he took comfort
in the fact that even then the Lord knew his path (although
the enemy had set snares right in his path - Psa.142:3). He
states emphatically in Psa.1:6 "The LORD knows the way of
the righteous", and in Psa.139:3, "You encompass my path,
and are acquainted with all my ways", and in Psa.91:11-12
"He shall give His angels charge over you, to keep you in
all your ways. In their hands they shall bear you up, lest you
dash your foot against a stone". Psa.56:13 – "Have You not
kept my feet from falling that I may walk before God…?"
"You enlarged my path under me, so my feet did not slip"
(Psa.18:36). "The law of God is in his heart; none of his
steps shall slide" (Psa.37:31).

The following scriptures remind us that walking on God's
path requires a decision and a commitment to holy living.
Prov.4:20-27 was written to a young man, but is wise counsel
for every one of us i.e. guard our hearts diligently; ponder
our path; remove our feet from evil. Psa.119:59, 101, 133

focuses on the importance of God's word in directing our footsteps; and Psa.73:1-3, 23-28 warns against getting our eyes off God, and becoming envious of the wicked who are prosperous, *until* ... see v.17!

22

A DIFFERENT WALK

"*W*hen Abram was ninety-nine years old, the Lord appeared to Abram and said to him, 'I am Almighty God; *walk before me and be blameless / perfect*'." Do you suppose Abram might have thought, "Hey, I'm only human! And I'm almost a hundred – give me a break already! Are You really talking to me, God? A covenant? Between me and El Shaddai? This is huge! You're going to multiply me? On your face, Abram! A father? I'm ninety-nine, and my wife's only ten years *less* old! Many nations, You say? I must be dreaming. A new name, too? Abraham – sort of rolls off the tongue. Circum-what? That doesn't sound pleasant! You're changing Sarai's name too? A mother? At ninety! Ha,ha,ha! There's Ishmael, You know. No? Isaac – that means 'Let him laugh' – well it *is* pretty funny". (Read what really happened in Genesis 17) The point is, God called Abraham to walk a different kind of walk, different from the world – *a walk of faith with Him*. Several generations later, another man was called by God to a different walk, and Moses brought Abraham's descendants, the Israelites, out of Egyptian slavery. Through Moses God gave instructions to Israel as to how they were to walk before Him. He said: "You shall observe My judgments and keep my ordinances to walk in them: I am the LORD your God' (Lev.18:4-5). "You shall walk in all the ways which the LORD your God has commanded you, *that you may live*, and that *it may be well with you...*" (Deut.5:33). "Fear the LORD your God,... walk in all His ways ...love Him ... serve the LORD your God with all your heart and with all your soul ... keep the commandments of the LORD and His statutes ... *for your good* " (Deut.10:12). God promised that if they obeyed Him, " The LORD will establish you as *a holy people to Himself* ... then all peoples of the earth shall see that *you are called by the name of the LORD*, and they shall be afraid of you" (Deut.28:9-10). See Deut.11:22-25.

Guess what – God is still calling out people who will walk in His ways, called by His name, to be a witness for Him. Remember that covenant with Abraham in Gen.12:1-3? In part it said "In you all the families of the earth shall be blessed". That includes us! Through Abraham's seed, Jesus Christ came to bring salvation to all who would believe, and to make us heirs to the blessing of Abraham, including the impartation of the Holy Spirit (Gal.3:13-14). Romans 8:1-4 is like a watershed. Read it carefully to get the full impact of the message. Christ came to free us from the law, which condemned us *in* our sin but could not save us *from* our sin. The sacrifice of Jesus, spotless Lamb of God, on our behalf, satisfied the demands of the law, which said, "The soul that sins shall die" (Ezek.18:20). On the cross, all the sin of all mankind was laid on Him, so when He died, it was for your sin and mine – it was as if we died with him (Rom.6; Gal.2:20). The penalty for sin was paid, so we were set free from the law's judgment. What does this mean as far as our 'walk' is concerned? If we are freed from the rules of the Mosaic Law, which no one could keep in totality, what is our code of living? If there is no more condemnation under the law, does that mean the rules are out the window? What does Rom.8:1-4 say? The law, which had no power to make us righteous, has been replaced by the law of the Spirit of life, in Christ Jesus. The law brought death. The Holy Spirit brings life, and the ability to fulfill the law in us. We're not striving any longer by our own efforts to satisfy the demands of the law; as we yield to the Spirit, He will fulfill the righteousness of the law in us.

So what should *our* walk look like? This 'list' is not exhaustive, nor in any order of importance, but each one is an indication that we walk in God's path, a 'different' path in the best sense of the word. It is a <u>walk in newness of life</u>. This new life is a result of a new birth into God's family (John 3:3; 1:12). It is Christ's life in us by His Spirit (Col.1:27; 2 Cor.5:17). I want to say at the outset, the walk we are to walk is not based on a set of rules for us to work on, in a self-effort to appear to be a good Christian. That only leads to self-righteousness and hypocrisy, which may fool people, but not God, who sees the heart. God gave us His Spirit to do the work of transformation in us, and our part is to give Him permission to do this, with repentance from dead works and inward sin being the first step in letting Him have the reins (Phil.2:13; 1:6). Having said that, the whole focal point, from which everything else emanates, is that we <u>walk in the Spirit</u>. Unless we are yielded to the Spirit, we cannot walk in a way that is pleasing to God. Rom.8:1 tells us "There is now ... no condemnation to those who ... do not walk according to the flesh, but according to the Spirit." Ergo, what is not done in the Spirit is dead works of the flesh, which brings condemnation (Rom.8:5-11). If we are walking in the Spirit, our lives will display the fruit of the Spirit (Gal.5:16-25; John 15:1-8). The new commandment of Jesus to His followers is "Love one another as I have loved you" (John 13:34). We are commanded to "<u>Walk in love</u>" (Eph.5:2; 2 John 5-6). This love cannot be manufactured in our human emotional factory. It is "the love of God (that) has been poured out in our hearts by the Holy Spirit" (Rom.5:5). Love is the Spirit's fruit, God's love producing the fruit of love in us. We will not bear fruit unless we receive His love (Eph.3:14-19).

We began our walk by faith in Christ for our salvation from sin, so it is only natural that we continue to "walk in ... faith" (Rom.4:12) and to "walk by faith, not by sight" (2 Cor.5:7). "If we walk in the light as He is in the light, we have fellowship with one another" (1 John 1:7). Jesus, the Light of the world (John 8:12), died to bring us out of darkness into light, and by walking in the light, the sin and evil in us is exposed and overcome (John 3:19-21; 11:9-10; 12:46; Eph.5:8, 11). Col.2:6-10 says "As you have received Christ Jesus the Lord, so walk in Him". Since Jesus is the Light, then walking in Christ means we are walking in the light. And because light dispels the works of darkness, it follows that we will walk honestly (KJV) (Rom.13:13; 1 Thes.4:12). If we are in Christ we will also walk in truth (2 John 4), because He is truth (John 14:6). Are you beginning to see that walking in the Spirit is the same as walking in Christ, because Christ is in us by His Spirit? (Gal.2:20) All of these commands are a natural outcome of living in Him and His living in us. Here are a few more to ponder: "Walk as He walked" (1 John 2:6; Eph.5:1). Walk in good works (Eph.2:10; Acts 10:38 – Jesus was anointed by the Holy Spirit in order to do good works). "Walk in wisdom" (Col.4:5; 1:9; 2:2-3). "Walk carefully (circumspectly-KJV)" (Eph.5:15-17; 1Pet.5:8). "Walk worthy of the Lord" (Col.1:10). "Walk worthy of (your) calling" (Eph.4:1; 1 Cor.1:2- as *saints*; Rom.8:29-30; 15-17 – *as children of God, and heirs with Christ*.) "Walk in the fear of the Lord and the comfort of the Holy Spirit" (Acts 9:31). And, those who walk with Him faithfully now "shall walk with (Him) in white, for they are worthy" (Rev.3:4).

23

WALKING IN TRUTH

𝕾𝕺

*W*hen Pilate asked Jesus at His mockery of a trial, "What is truth?" little did he know he was looking Truth in the eye, yet somehow he knew that truly this man before him was innocent of any crime. To his credit, he tried to release Jesus as a result. But it was for this moment of imminent death that Jesus was born, and nothing could hush the voices of His accusers. When John wrote about Jesus' entrance onto the world stage, he said, "Grace and truth came through Jesus Christ" (John 1:17). Not many years later, as Jesus' Spirit-anointed ministry of teaching and healing was drawing to a close, He told His disciple, Thomas, "I am the Way, the Truth and the Life" (John 14:6). How strange these words must have sounded to those who heard! The position of the words in His statement, suggests that Truth is what connects the other two words. *Truth* is the *Way* to *Life*. They are all bound up together to express Jesus' purpose for being here among men. John also wrote in John 1:1, that Jesus is the Word, eternal God in the beginning, who took on flesh and dwelt among us. He came to teach us Truth, to show us the Father, and by His death to open the Way to eternal Life. When Jesus returned to the Father after His resurrection, He sent the Spirit of Truth to live in all who accept Him by faith, promising that His Spirit would guide us into all Truth (John 16:13). Jesus is the Life-giving Word of Truth for all mankind! Only as we know the Truth (Jesus) do we find the Way to Live, to be all we can possibly be, freed from our past, completely fulfilled, and fulfilling God's purpose, and prepared for an everlasting reign with Him. Jesus, the Truth, gives us Life, through His Spirit living in us. This makes us bearers of the Truth indeed! A popular expression in our day is, "You haven't lived until you" ... do this or that, go here or there, see or hear or taste or feel something that is somebody's notion of the ultimate sensual experience. The truth is we don't really live until we are made alive in Christ, and then all these other things pale in comparison.

Why is this Truth so important, so vital, and so necessary for Life? Jesus said that we would know the Truth, and the *Truth would make us free* (John 8:32). No other message, no other religion, no other proclamation, can set us free – free from sin, death, and our past; free from fear, guilt and shame; free from condemnation and judgment; free to live in joy and peace and love; free to be who we were created to be. Jesus also said that we are *sanctified by the Truth of the word* (Eph.5:25b-27; John 17:17). It is the truth of Jesus, in His word, that transforms us, by renewing our mind, in reality forming the mind of Christ in us, as we hear, speak and meditate on His amazing truth (Rom.12:2).

Just what are some of the truths that we need to know? God, through the prophet Hosea lamented, "My people are destroyed for lack of knowledge". Jesus echoed similar words, when He said to the Jewish religious leaders, "You will not come to Me (the Truth), that you might have life" (John 5:38-40). Some of the basic truths of the Word that we need to know for Life are the truth about:

1) the Godhead – His character, His works, His plan of salvation

2) ourselves – who we are, and who God wants us to be in Him;

3) sin - its consequences, and its cure through the blood of Christ;

4) salvation, repentance, sanctification, and holy living;

5) our enemy, Satan, and the reality of spiritual warfare;

6) heaven and hell, angels and demons, wonders and miracles;

7) the gifts of the Holy Spirit to the church and in our lives.

We need to know that just because we believe something, or were taught something, and are convinced of its verity in our minds, this does not mean it is truth. Truth is not relative. It is absolute or it is not truth. It becomes a lie, fiction, fable, fantasy, or delusion. In our culture, we are taught these from early childhood. Cartoon characters, fairies, mermaids and mythical creatures, monsters, aliens, the Easter bunny and Santa Claus, Pokemon, and his ilk, etc. are presented to our minds as truth. In our schools we are taught <u>lies from the pit of hell</u>:

1) that we were not created by God, in His image, for his glory, with an eternal soul;

2) that we evolved from simple life forms (*so we can boast of how far we have come*);

3) that we are just a higher, more intelligent form of animals (*and we live like them*);

4) that we do not have to answer to God for how we live, since there is no God anyway.

We've heard people say, "That couldn't be farther from the truth!" If the truth were told, even the slightest deviation from the truth means it is no longer truth. This is especially the case in regards to the Gospel of Truth, which the Apostle Paul received by revelation from Jesus Himself (Ga.1:12), and was commissioned to proclaim, first to the Jews, but mainly to the Gentiles. This was Gospel Truth – the two words are really synonymous. But from the beginning of the proclamation of the Gospel of the Grace of God, there have been hundreds (thousands? millions?) of people who have taught and preached 'another gospel'. This has been done in a number of ways, a few of which are:

1) perverting the truth (that is misusing, misinterpreting, or diverging from the truth (2 Pet.2;1-3);

2) embellishing or adding error to the truth (Rev.22:18) (adulteration of the truth);

3) subtracting from the truth (Rev.22:19) (refuting parts of the truth);

4) watering down the truth to make it more acceptable to the hearers (2 Tim.4:3-4).

It behooves every minister of the Gospel today to preach "the Truth, the whole Truth, and nothing but the Truth." See Galatians 1:6-10. Jesus is the embodiment of truth. There was never a hint of deception in Him – no duplicity, no hypocrisy, no flattering words, and no compromise. This is why people were attracted to Him. This is why the believers down through the centuries have been willing to die for this Truth. They were absolutely committed to the Truth, because they knew beyond any doubt that this was for real, and their very lives depended on it. Dear ones, <u>our lives</u> also depend on the Truth of the Gospel, which is so evidently set forth in the letters to the churches, and to us. It is time to study the Word, not just depending on what we hear from others, but letting the Spirit of Truth Himself teach us and guide us into all Truth! This is the truth Jesus said would set us free, but only if we know Him, who is the truth, and obey His words!

24

WHO IS THE HOLY SPIRIT?

*M*y encounter a few weeks ago with the truth of Galatians 3:13-14, concerning God's promise of His Spirit to all nations through His covenant with Abraham, brought me to a topic that could be very difficult to address. I wonder how many thousands of books and articles have been written, from almost as many viewpoints, about the Holy Spirit. Who / what is the Holy Spirit? And do we even need to discuss the topic? I believe the importance of the Holy Spirit becomes obvious when we realize that from the very beginning of the record of man in the book of Genesis, till the very end of that record, in Revelation, He is there. Gen.1:2 declares that "the Spirit of God was hovering over the face of the waters". He was present at creation, in fact was the power that brought the universe into being, at the will of the Father, and the word of the Son. And at the end of time as we know it, He is calling people through the church to "Come, and receive the water of life" (Rev.22:17). Throughout the Scriptures, His presence and work is manifested in the lives of people, in particular but not exclusively among the chosen Israelite nation, and later in the called-out church. It might be near impossible to take an honest look at the scriptures and come up with unbiased truth. It is not my intention to present arguments from any position, but just to let the Word speak for itself, and thus impact our hearts and lives.

Last year, a dear friend blessed me with a copy of the New Spirit Filled Life Bible, for which I am very thankful. At the beginning of each book, along with facts about the writer, dates, content and personal application, are comments on how Christ is revealed, and how the Holy Spirit is shown to be at work throughout the book. This has been so helpful in my understanding of the Word, especially the Old Testament, and of the Holy Spirit revealed therein. For example, in Genesis, the heathen King Pharaoh recognized God's Spirit at work in the life of Joseph (Gen.41:38). In the book of Numbers, the Spirit of the Lord that was upon Moses was passed on to elders from each tribe, who began to prophesy (Num.11:17, 25). The Holy Spirit was given credit for words spoken by the prophet Ezekiel (Ezek.11:5), and even for stirring up King Cyrus of Persia to allow God's people to return to their homeland, and to assist them on the journey (Ezra 1:1-4). Often in some of the books the Spirit of God is not mentioned, yet His work is seen in the lives of God's people and on their behalf in the face of their enemies.

Let us get back to the question of the identity of the Holy Spirit. Right off the top we need to know that He is God (Acts 5:3-5), not an 'it'. He is not an influence, though He does influence and persuade people (John 16:8-11); not a force, though He does give mighty power to people (Judg.15:14); and not a created being like angels or people. He was present at creation, and one of the 'us' in the words "Let Us make man in Our image" (Gen.1:26). He is a person in the sense that He has personality, the ability to think and act, and has power and authority in the lives of believers. He was the person whose life was breathed into the nostrils of Adam, coming to live in him, to produce the life of God within him

(Gen.2:7). It was His life that was removed from Adam's spirit when Adam sinned by disobeying God's command, thus breaking the fellowship between God and man. And it is when we receive life through the Holy Spirit in the New Birth, and His life is in us, that this communion with the Godhead is restored, and we are called the children of God (John 1:12-13; Eph.1:5; Titus 3:5-7; Rom.8:14-16).

Hebrews 9:14 describes the Holy Spirit as "the eternal Spirit", and links Him with God the Father, and the Son, as a member of the Godhead. This connection is also referred to in 1 Cor.2:10-11, where He is called the Spirit of God and the Spirit who is from God, who knows the deep things of God. (Note: We have come to know the Godhead as the Trinity, or the Triune God although these are not Biblical terms.) 1 John 5:7 shows the unity of the Father, the Word (Jesus) and the Holy Spirit. Matt.28:19 gives instructions concerning baptism "in the name of the Father and of the Son and of the Holy Spirit". Paul closes his second letter to the Corinthians by writing, "The grace of the Lord Jesus Christ, and the love of God, and the communion of the Holy Spirit be with you all." There is no indication in any of these references, that any one person of the Godhead is any less important or of lower status than any of the others. We have already seen that they have different roles to play, all of which are essential in the universe, and in the lives of God's people.

Many have tried to illustrate the concept of 'One God in three persons'. For example, in describing the sun, we could say the sun is light. We could also say the sun is heat, or that it is energy. In reality the sun is all of these, or at least a source of all three. At the same time, it is still one sun, and separating its heat from its light, or any one of its components from any other of its components does not in any way negate that it is still the sun. Every component is vital to life

115

on earth, and we need it in all its fullness. Similarly, we walk in the light of the Word (the Son), soak in the warmth of the Father's love and provision, and do exploits in the power of the Holy Spirit. It is vital to our life as a believer that we are in intimate fellowship with God the Father, God the Son and God the Holy Spirit. Otherwise, we cannot experience the abundant life Jesus offers (John 10:10). Receive His Abundant Life today!

Please refer back to this teaching in chapter two, which shows that each Person of the Godhead is a strand in the threefold cord that is the antidote to fear. This is just one example of the need to know each One personally, and to be yielded to the will of the Father, doers of the Word, and tuned in and obedient to the voice of the Holy Spirit. The three persons are <u>one</u> in thought, word and action; they cannot and will not contradict each other. Each is equally important. If we constantly talk about, and pray to Jesus only, we do not comprehend the amazing Father-love that created us for His pleasure, and wants to lavish every good and perfect gift on us. Jesus Himself said we were not to ask Him for anything, but to ask the Father, in Jesus' name (John 16:23-24). If we only talk about God, and never mention Jesus, do we even understand that Jesus is the only way to the Father, and He died that we might live? Whenever the Holy Spirit is overlooked or relegated to an occasional passing mention, the power is missing, and the Galatian syndrome chokes out the abundant life in the Spirit (Gal.3:3). Where the Holy Spirit is glorified above the Word and the Father, with an overemphasis on the spiritual <u>gifts</u>, instead of a focus on love, obedience, and the <u>fruit</u> of the Spirit, confusion reigns (1 Cor.12-14) and the witness is negated.

25

THE WORK OF
THE HOLY SPIRIT

F or years, even decades, after I was born again, I didn't
really understand who the Holy Spirit is, or how much
I need Him in order to live the abundant life Jesus promised. In the four different churches I have attended, it was
as if the subject of the Holy Spirit was too hot to handle.
It was the same at Bible school. We were warned against
extremism, and anything that involved miracles of healing
(they were staged!), of tongues (they were fake!), and Spirit
baptism (was it even addressed?) I never understood or
experienced the reality, the power or the abiding presence
of the Holy Spirit in my life. I tried to show the fruit of the
Spirit, and worked really hard to please God, but failed
miserably. I hated my hypocrisy, my hidden sins, and my
lack of joy. Then, a couple of years ago I was given a little
paperback book authored by Catherine Marshall, entitled
"The Helper". (Thank God for friends who listen to the Holy
Spirit's promptings!) All the truths about the Holy Spirit that
had just been words on a page became real in my life, as
I learned I could ask the Father for the filling and baptism
of His Spirit. The Holy Spirit longs to do His work in us,

but cannot if we crowd Him out with dead works of self-righteousness, hidden sins and the things of this world (1 Thes.5:19; Eph.4:30-32; 1 John 2:15-16). Be reminded that dead works need to be repented of and cast off (Heb.6:1; 9:14), as well as hidden sins (2 Cor.4:2).

Even before we are born again, the Holy Spirit works in us to bring conviction of sin, preparing us to accept the righteousness of Christ, Who broke Satan's power at the cross (John 16:8-11). The Holy Spirit births us into God's family (John 3:5-6) by bringing His life into our spirit (Rom.8:9). His Spirit confirms to us that we are God's child, and can call God 'Abba' (Daddy), and are guaranteed heirs to all His riches (Rom.8:15-17; Eph.1:13-14)! But He doesn't put a stamp on us, then leave us on our own. Just before Jesus went to the cross, and his disciples were already beginning to feel deserted and alone, He promised them that after His death and resurrection, when He returned to the Father in heaven, He would send to them the same Spirit that was in Him during His time on earth. It would be just as if HE, Jesus, was with them - even better, because the Holy Spirit was not restricted by a body, and would dwell in each of them, and in all who were born again, and would never leave them alone. He would be their teacher, to lead them into all truth, from Jesus' words, and all scripture (John 16:13-15; 1 John 2:27). It's amazing how those 'difficult, meaningless' passages in God's word come alive to us in life-changing ways as we let the Holy Spirit be our teacher! You see, Jesus promised the indwelling Holy Spirit to us as well as to those disciples, to do in us the same works that Jesus did, and even greater works! (John14:12)

As believers, indwelt by the Spirit of God, we need to know that He has been given to us to be not only a teacher, but also a helper. The word translated 'helper' suggests someone called alongside, to be an intercessor, comforter, helper, advocate, counselor (John 14:26; John 15:26). He leads us, gives us direction, warns us, and puts a check in our spirit when we should not do something (Rom.8:14; Acts 13:4; Acts 16:6). He gives us the words to speak in times of need (Luke 12:11-12). He wars against our fleshly desires, empowering us to overcome the evil within us (Gal.5:16-17; 1 John 4:4; Isa.59:19). He completes the work of sanctification in our souls (Gal.3:3). He works through His gifts to edify the church, and produces His good fruit in our lives (1 Cor.12; 13; 14; Gal.5:22-23). His anointing empowers us for witness and ministry (Acts 1:8; 2 Cor.1:21; Luke 4:18).

The Holy Spirit was present throughout the life of Jesus, right from birth (Luke 1:35). At His water baptism, He was *baptized by the Holy Spirit*, an anointing for the ministry He was about to begin (John 1:33; Matt.3:16). If Jesus, the perfect Son of man, needed the anointing of the Holy Spirit for His ministry, how much more do we need it? Does it make you wonder if the reason why so many ministries fail, there is so much burn out, and people in ministry fall into immoral or unethical behavior is because so much of their so-called ministry is done in the power of the flesh? Could it be they have never had an anointing of the Spirit to give them power, impetus, wisdom and strength? Think of what Jesus said to the believers after His resurrection. He had just breathed on them, transferring into them the Spirit that was in Him (John 20:22). And yet, later on, He told them "Behold, I send the Promise of My Father upon you; but tarry in the city of Jerusalem until you are endued with power from on high." (Luke 24:49) In Acts 1:5 Jesus reminded them of John's words at His baptism, and said "John truly baptized with water, but you shall be baptized with the Holy Spirit not many days from now". He continues in verse 8 "You shall receive *power* when the Holy Spirit is come upon you, and you shall be witnesses to Me....to the end of the earth". Did you catch the different prepositions here? Is having the Spirit living *in* us the same as Him coming *upon* us?

We have already seen that at Salvation the Holy Spirit comes into our Spirit, and dwells there as a witness to us that we are children of God. But Jesus said that in order to receive power, we need the Holy Spirit to come upon us. He used the word 'baptism', making it distinct from water baptism, although they can happen at the same time (Acts 8:14-17; 19:5-6). The word baptism means to be immersed, enveloped, whelmed. Water is often used as a picture of the Holy Spirit, especially an abundance of rushing, powerful water (John 7:38-39). We can think of our spirit as a receptacle, such as a glass, to receive the Holy Spirit, who can flow into us, and also overflow out of us to others. What if we were to take that glass and immerse it in the ocean, so that the water in the glass, and all around the glass becomes one? How much more power there is now, in us, and upon us! Now, we are controlled completely by that power. We are not operating in our own strength, but yield to wherever the Holy Spirit leads us in His power. Those disciples, who received the Holy Spirit from Jesus, did not have power for their ministry until the Spirit came upon them in baptism at Pentecost. And then they were radically changed immediately, becoming bold witnesses who astounded the whole city of Jerusalem and beyond with their preaching and living. Let us be very careful not to dictate what the Holy Spirit can or cannot do. We need to allow Him to do His will in us, even if it is not comfortable!

Do you think it is natural for someone who is born supernaturally by the Spirit of God, into the family of God, is forgiven of all his sin, and will someday be taken to heaven somewhere, be given a new body that won't deteriorate or die, and live with God forever, to live a life devoid of any evidence of the *supernatural* life??? Watch Him surprise and amaze you, over and over again! Say good-bye to boring; say hello to exciting!

26

IS THE FRUIT GROWING?

"The fruit of the Spirit is love..." Gal.5:22-23

I love fruit! Some of my fondest memories from childhood are of summer hours spent picking berries – the tiny flavor-packed strawberries along the railroad tracks, and in the wooded areas around the sloughs; in the river valleys, the fat, purple saskatoons that filled our buckets, and later our bellies with their goodness; and the soft, juicy raspberries, plucked from thorny bushes and handled with gentle care. But I also loved the wooden boxes of fruit shipped in from warmer spots, each peach or pear wrapped in tissue paper, and hidden in their crate under the bed until they were ripe enough to go into jars for the winter ahead. Tropical fruits were rare in our home then, but now pineapples, papayas, passion fruit, mangoes, and kiwis are among my favorites. One thing I've learned is that you only get one kind of fruit from a tree, and every tree is unique.

So it's always puzzled me that the Bible talks about the *fruit* (singular) of the Spirit, and then proceeds to name nine different varieties (Gal.5:22-23). Is it fruit or are they fruits?? Maybe it's a package deal, all or nothing? Or could it be a progressive fruit, where one sort of grows out of the previous one; or they all sprout out from love like octopus arms? (I just found out that an octopus has six arms and two legs – it would be fun to have six arms!) I kind of like the idea of everything being an offshoot of love. Love's the most important fruit, and we really need to have <u>love</u> before anything else happens. I also appreciate the fact that all these good qualities / characteristics are called fruit, not vegetable or grain, just because fruit is special! (And here endeth the levity – some 325 words later!).

The fruit of the Spirit (Gal.5:22-23) is especially attractive compared to those 'nasties' listed in the previous verses (19-21). Aren't you glad those things aren't called fruit? That would denigrate the whole fruit family! The works of the flesh – these are works of the natural person, the one not born of the Spirit. These 'works' manifest what is in the heart of an unregenerate person, who cannot "inherit the kingdom of God." Conversely, the fruit of the Spirit manifests what *should be* in the heart of one who is born again, regenerated by the Spirit of God. If we are manifesting some of those fleshly works instead of the Spirit's fruit (maybe just things like envy or anger or hatred), then we bring dishonor to the Lord we profess to follow, and denigrate His Name and His whole family.

There are at least two possible reasons why a believer's life does not manifest love, joy, peace, etc. One is that we are trying in our own efforts to grow this fruit, and it is just plain fake. Fruit is not produced by works. It is the natural result of a healthy tree. Jesus said, "I am the vine, you are the branches. He who abides in me, and I in him, bears much fruit, for without me you can do nothing." (John 15:5) Is Christ abiding in you by His Spirit, and are you rooted and grounded in Him, so the life of the Vine will flow through you to produce the beautiful fruit of righteousness? If not, repent of those dead works, cease striving, and yield to the Holy Spirit, allowing Him to till and water the hard soil of your heart, and shine the light of His glory in to dispel the darkness of unbelief and doubt; and in that light the blossoms and fruit of the Spirit will grow, blessing us and the lives of others we meet.

Another reason for fruitlessness could be that the thorns of the cares of the world or hidden sins are choking the life from the branches (Matt.13:22). Let the Holy Spirit do some pruning, uprooting those destructive thorns, cutting off dead branches and removing debris in you that hinders the flow of the sap (John 15:1-2). Then His love and its companions will begin to grow and manifest in you, replacing bitterness and its cohorts. How beautiful is a life filled with the fruit of the Spirit! It is a beauty that grows from the inside out, and is more lovely and attractive than what any salon could produce. Even before the fruit begins to grow, the sweet perfume of the blossoms "diffuses the fragrance of His knowledge in every place" (2 Cor.2:14-16), all for the glory of God!

It just hit me that if we read the description of love in 1 Cor.13, we just might find that each of the other fruit(s) of the Spirit is part of the definition of love. I wonder if Gal.5:22-23 should have been written something like this: "The fruit of the Spirit is love (i.e. joy, peace, patience, kindness, gentleness, goodness, faithfulness, self-control)". Let's compare the two passages.

1. Joy Love "rejoices in the truth" (v.6)

2. Peace Love "does not seek its own, is not provoked" (v.5)

3. Patience "Love suffers long", "endures all things" (v4, 7)

4. <u>Kindness</u> Love "is kind" (v.4)

5. <u>Gentleness</u> Love "bears all things"

6. <u>Goodness</u> Love "thinks no evil" (v.5)

7. <u>Faithfulness</u> "Love never fails" (v.8)

8. <u>Self-control</u> Love "does not behave rudely" (v.5)

Love is *all* of these things. They are all *components* of love. The fruit (singular) of the Spirit is LOVE. I believe that is the answer to the grammatical inconsistency I obsessed over at the beginning of this chapter. The fruit of the Spirit is love in all of its facets. ONE FRUIT = LOVE. (I need to make a disclaimer here – I am not suggesting another revision of the Scriptures to accommodate this amazing discovery, but if anyone is in the process, they might want to change some punctuation in Gal.5:22-23.)

Did you ever bite into a fruit you'd never tasted before, and try to describe it? You might think something like this about the fruit called love: "Wow, I just got a mouthful of <u>meekness</u> (KJV) / (gentleness). Now this piece is like ... <u>peace</u>. That one gave me a jolt of <u>joy</u>. Mmmmm ... <u>goodness</u>. This feels like <u>faithfulness</u>. I can't wait for the next bite – ah – <u>patience</u>! Now this is kind of like ... <u>kindness</u>. Of *course* the last bite is <u>self-control</u>. It probably wanted to be first!" You see, when we show love, it is displayed in any one of these ways, but it is still love. Love is what people see and feel when we are gentle and kind and patient, etc. And remember, it's the fruit of the Spirit, not some artificial facsimile that we might try to pass off as the real thing. Make sure you have the genuine goods, "the love of God ... poured out in our hearts by the Holy Spirit who was given to us" (Rom.5:5).

You have been chosen to bear fruit (John15:16), but you cannot display the Spirit's fruit in your life unless you are abiding in the Vine (Jesus), and His Spirit is abiding in you (John 15:4-5).

STUDY THREE

A NEW SONG

Psalm 40:3

27

A SONG OF DELIVERANCE

𝕾𝕾

*"The ransomed of the Lord shall ... come ...
with singing"*. (Isa.51:11)

*H*ave you ever noticed that people who know they have
been redeemed out of the kingdom of darkness, and
brought into the Kingdom of Light, are people who sing?
After the Israelites had crossed the Red Sea on dry ground,
and then watched as their pursuers were swallowed up when
the sea flowed back, they burst into song, led by Moses, in
praise to the LORD (Exod.15:1-18). It was a *new* song, one
they could not have sung just a few days earlier, as they were
enslaved in cruel bondage in Egypt. Now they were free, and
on their way to the rest and abundance of the land God had
promised to Abraham hundreds of years earlier. Fast forward
a few centuries, to the return of the Babylonian captives to
the same land, and see their joyful singing expressed in the
words of Psa.126. Both of these events are pictures of how
God has redeemed *us*, delivering us first of all from the penalty of sin, and then from the bondage that comes (sometimes over and over again) when we listen to the voice of
the enemy, and let our minds become captivated by his lies.
Both deliverances are cause for singing. The good news is,

it is God Himself who puts a new song in our mouths, and in our hearts, a song of praise to our great Savior! (Psa.40:3; Col.3:16) These songs of God have been sung since creation (Job 38:4, 7), in the Old Testament tabernacle worship (1 Chron.6:31-32; Psa.100:2; 66:2; 68:24-25), in times of trouble (Psa.32:7; 144:9), by angels at Jesus' birth (Luke 2:13), by godly women (Judg.5; Luke 1:46-55), in prison (Acts16:25), and by the church (Eph.5:19; 1 Cor.14:15). And they will be sung by the saints and angels in heaven (Rev.5:9; 15:3).

One thing about these songs from God that sets them apart from the songs of the world, is that they focus, not on *us and our* accomplishments, but on His boundless love, His matchless grace, His unfailing mercy, His singular goodness and mighty power. They laud His pure holiness and indescribable glory (Rev.4:8-11). His songs are based on His Word (Psa.119:54), such as are numerous hymns and songs we sing today. How many of the Psalms exhort us to sing songs of praise to our God, as David did all through his life! (Psa.33:1-3) David said "in the night His song shall be with me" (Psa.42:8), even when his soul was cast down, and he felt oppressed and anxious. After the Lord delivered David from Saul and other enemies, he sang a powerful song of deliverance to God, recorded in 2 Sam.22 and Psa.18. He closes with the words: "Therefore I will give thanks to You, O LORD, among the Gentiles, and sing praises to Your name." When I read David's Psalms, I always feel glad when even though at the beginning of a psalm there is frequently a lot of 'complaining' prayer, at the end the praise to God explodes out of the song that God had put in his heart. What I really love are the Psalms that begin with thanksgiving, and build into a crescendo of praise and exaltation that gives my heart wings and makes my lips sing along. "Oh that *we* would praise the LORD for His goodness, and for His wonderful works to the children of men!" I was just glancing at the opening words of some of the Psalms, and these are ones that say "Oh come, let us sing unto the LORD!" (95), "Oh, sing to the LORD a new song!" (96, 98) and "Praise the LORD!" (106, 111, 112, 113, 117, 135, 146 -150).

What I am curious about is whether we are singing this new song of praise and deliverance, not just during 'worship' time at church, but throughout all our days, 24-7. The reason I wonder is because I see among God's people the furrowed brows, the fearful, gloomy countenances, the dejected postures. I hear murmuring and complaining, words of strife, accusation, anger and bitterness. I discern spirits of unforgiveness, self-pity, jealousy and accusation. For some reason, it is my understanding that what is evident on the outside is a reflection of what is on the inside (Matt.12:34-35; Jas.3:14-18). Has the heart-song been silenced because we are grieving the Holy Spirit? (Eph.4:30. Read vs.22-32; Jas.4:7-10). I will always remember the transformation that took place in my spirit, and subsequently in every area of my life, when I began to repent of and renounce the hidden works of darkness within me (2 Cor.4:2). Every attitude, action, belief and emotion that was *not of God* had to go. Some of these had come into me through my generations, and even through legalistic teaching in the church. As I released these, received God's forgiveness, and cast out the spirits behind them, the tears of repentance were immediately turned into songs of praise, with laughter coming out of an inner joy, peace and freedom. This is the reason Jesus came! (Isa.61:1-3; Luke 4:16-21) He has given us the song of deliverance, but we will only be able to sing it if our heart is in tune with *His* heart (1 John 1:3-2:5). When we sing this song in our heart, it will be evident in our life. Ergo, "Many will *see it* and fear, and will trust in the LORD." (Psa.40:3)

Are people attracted to Christ because of the new song in your heart?

Let's revisit the Psalms to see how the beloved musician made the shift from sadness to song. David recognized that his depression, burdens, guilt, troubles and physical ailments (Psa.32:3-4) were a result of unconfessed sin (Psa.38:1-4ff), past iniquities (Psa.40:12), and sins of his youth (Psa.25:7, 11, 17-18). He realized that his only hope of deliverance was in the LORD against whom he had sinned (Psa.51:4; 40:11, 13). David's spirit was broken over his sins, and his heart was contrite (v.17). So he acknowledged his sins (Psa.38:18; 51:3-4), repented of them, and asked God for His forgiveness (Psa.51:1-2, 7, 9-10). Then He asked the LORD to give him back His song! (vs.8, 12, 14-15) *Only then* would his witness bring sinners to the LORD (v.13). David's testimony of repentance and a restored song is recorded in Psa.32:1-2, 5-8, 11. Perhaps this experience made David realize that God already knows everything about us (Psa.139:1-18; Psa.69:5; Heb.4:13), and that He wants us to have a pure heart. As a result he prayed for God to search his heart, so that he (David) would know what was there, in order to repent of his sin (Psa.139:23-24). In Psa.19:12-14, he prayed that God would cleanse him from secret faults, and keep him from presumptuous/willful sins. He knew in his heart that it is the Word of God that will keep our thoughts and speech pure, as we meditate on it and apply it to our lives (Psa.1:1-2; 19:7-11; 119:1-3, 9, 104, and 133).

Satan wants us to *hide* our sins (2 Cor.4:4). But God wants to *reveal* our sins to us by the light of His Spirit through the Word, in order that we can find grace, forgiveness and healing (Psa.90:8; 2 Pet.3:9; Rom.2:4-5). We are reminded in Heb.4:12-16 that His word convicts of the sin God sees within us, not to condemn us, but so we will come to Him for mercy. Don't downplay or negate the need for repentance, turning away from things that defile us and bind us. It will restore the joy and bring back the song God gave us! Let the song ring out! Let the light shine!

28

SALT AND LIGHT

"You are the salt of the earth." – Matt.5:13

"You are the light of the world." – Matt.5:14

*W*hen God chose Abraham and his descendents to be His chosen people, His purpose was to bless all nations of the earth through them (Gen.12:2-3). They were to be a witness to the Gentiles of the greatness and glory of Jehovah God. Every time He miraculously delivered them from the tyranny and bondage of their enemies, He was showing them that He is the LORD (Exod.7:5; 9:13-16; 14:18; Josh.2:10-11). Israel was also to show the Gentiles a God who is holy, righteous and just, but also merciful and forgiving, who blesses those who trust in Him and obey His word. So how did they do with this mandate? The prophet Hosea describes in detail the unfaithfulness and sins of Israel and Judah, and says, "Israel is swallowed up. Now they are among the Gentiles like a vessel in which is no pleasure" (Hos.8:8). Ezekiel's indictment is even more scathing, declaring that the house of Israel had profaned the LORD's holy name among the nations wherever they went (Ezek.36:22). Jeremiah devoted most of a long book to weeping over the transgressions of God's people, who had forsaken the LORD, and become in their iniquities and idolatry worse than the nations to which they were called to be a light (Jer.2:7-8; 13:27; 19:4-5; 23:11-14. See 2 Kings 21:9). This all happened because they chose to be *like* those nations, worshipping their gods, adopting their ways, intermarrying with them, making treaties with them, forsaking the LORD who loved them, and forgetting the covenant He made with them (2 Kings 17:7-17). But God did not forsake them, and He remembered His covenant with them (Jer.3:12-15; 16:14-15; 29:10-13; 30:2-3). In His mercy and grace, He will restore them, through the One He sent to be the Light of the World (John1:1-5). Because of Jesus, once again Israel will be a light to the Gentiles (Isa.42:6; 60:1-3; 62:1-2; 66:19b; Rom.11:26-27).

In Isa.49:6 the LORD speaks concerning the coming Messiah, "I will also give You as a light to the Gentiles, that You should be My salvation to the ends of the earth." Jesus was that light (John 8:12), and He said, "He who follows Me ... shall have the light of life". In His famous message to the multitudes on the mountain, He told His disciples, "*You* are the light of the world. Let your light so shine before men, that they may see your good works and glorify your Father in heaven" (Matt.5:14-16 - we are not to hide our light, but let it be seen by all). We are also called sons of light (Luke 16:8, 1 Thes.5:5), light in the Lord and children of light (Eph.5:8), and are told we are to shine as lights in the midst of a crooked and perverse generation (Phil.2:15). So how are *we* doing with this mandate from the One who gave us His light as well as His song? We need to realize that the light in us is not our own light. In reality, it is the light of the burning oil of the Holy Spirit, a light which we are commanded not to quench (1 Thes.5:19). If this unquenched light were to shine out from all God's people, imagine how it would dispel darkness, and bring the light and hope of salvation to those who stumble in darkness! Jesus once said that people who practice evil don't come to the light (John 3:19-20), but if *we* go to *them* with His light and His song, they will see our deeds (John 3:21), and be drawn to the true Light and to the Source of indescribable joy and song!

For a light to be effective, it needs to be seen, like a city on a hill, or a lamp on a stand, not a candle hidden under a basket (Jesus' words in Matt.5:14-16). Maybe we are hiding our light in the closet, or saving it for Sundays only, in church, where we feel safe among the other feeble flickering lights. It reminds me of the disciples gathered in the upper room, waiting for the baptism of the Holy Spirit (Acts 1:4-5, 12-14). When the Holy Spirit came upon them on the Day of Pentecost, they were lit with His fire, and thrust out into the throng of people that had gathered at the sound of the excitement (Acts 2:1-6). Their light and their song were irresistible, as each person in the crowd heard the Gospel of Grace in his own language, preached by these radically changed disciples who were "uneducated and untrained men" (Acts 4:13). That day three thousand people came to the Light, and in turn became lights in the world (Acts 2:41-42). May the Holy Spirit baptize *us* with His fire and send us out to bear the light and song to a dark and hurting world! (Acts 1:8)

In Jesus' teaching, He also told His disciples, "You are the salt of the earth" (Matt.5:13). Today, as I was listening to the news, the anchor man was talking to a female reporter who had that day interviewed a famous western singer, who is also a Christian. In trying to get a feel of things, he asked her how she felt about this renowned performer. Without hesitation, she exclaimed, "Oh, the salt of the earth!" She went on to say how gracious he was, and so different from most celebrities (i.e. He answered all her questions, and then asked her if there were any more questions.) She was obviously impressed. I was, too, because He had lived up to his calling to be salt in this earth. Why did that reporter say he was the salt of the earth? Why did Jesus call His followers the salt of the earth? How are we salt? Salt adds flavor and taste to food, making it palatable and pleasant, but should not make the food salty. Our lives in Christ add a flavor to the society we live in, our Christian character influencing the culture in a positive way, making it more pleasing (Col.4:6). Our obedience to God and our prayers bring blessing on the city and country we live in (2 Chron.7:14). Our Christian morals and standards influence our laws and governments as we stand for what is right, vote in leaders who are godly and wise, and pray for those in office (1 Tim.2:1-4). 2 Cor.2:14-15, although using a different analogy, explains it so well. "Thanks be to God who always leads us in triumph in Christ, and through us diffuses the fragrance (*savor*) of His knowledge in every place. For we are to God the fragrance (*savor*) of Christ among those who are being saved and among those who are perishing". God uses *us* as His salt-shaker so people will taste and see that He is good! (Psa. 34:8)

Salt is also used as a preservative to prevent decay and putrefaction. I am of the opinion that believers, by prayer and godly living, keep our world from complete moral degeneration and corruption, widespread vice, and crime pandemics, as we are faithful to wage warfare against the father of all evil, and his forces at work throughout the world (2 Cor.4:4; 10:4-6; Eph.6:11-12). I also believe that world economics and prosperity is a gauge of the influence that God's children have. God promised to bless the nation that honors Him and His people (Prov.11:11; 14:34; Psa.33:12; Gen.12:3). May we, through lives surrendered to the control of the Holy Spirit, never lose our flavor! Let us dispense His salt, shine His light, and broadcast His song!

29

A NEW LOVE SONG

I wonder what percentage of all songs ever written could
be classified as love songs. Love seems to be a very
popular theme, and probably has been from the beginning of
time. Tucked between the books of Ecclesiastes and Isaiah
in the Old Testament is 'The Song of Solomon', a portrait of
marital love, and a picture of the covenant love relationship
between Christ and His church. If you've read through the
Old Testament, you know that God was big on covenants. Of
the covenants that God made with Abraham and his descendents, some were conditional on Israel's obedience, while
others were like a gift, with no stipulations. In the preceding
chapter we saw Jeremiah's record of Israel's repeated rebellion, and defilement in contrast to the *unfailing love* and
mercy of their covenant-keeping God. God's covenant had
spelled out punishment for disobedience, and true to His
word, He brought trouble and hardship on them (Jer.30:12-
15). But because of His love for Israel (Jer.31:3), and His
covenant with David, He forgave their sins and restored
them to their land.

In chapter 31 of Jeremiah's prophecy, there is a sudden shift,
as God makes reference to a new covenant – a covenant

in which His law will be in their hearts, their sins will be forgotten, and they will all know Him (i.e. <u>a new intimacy with God</u>) (vs.31-37). Psa.96:1ff tells *all the earth* "Oh, sing to the LORD <u>a new song</u> ... bless His name, proclaim the good news of His salvation ... declare His glory *among the nations*." Isaiah joins in with declarations of "<u>new things</u>" and a new song of praise *from the ends of the earth* (Isa.42:9-10), referring back to the prophecy of the coming Messiah (vs.1-8). When Jesus broke into time and space several centuries later, He came to establish this new covenant, with the preaching of the kingdom of God (Luke 16:16), and through His shed blood which would take away sin (Luke 22:19-20; ref. Jer.31:34). And with the new covenant came <u>a new commandment</u>: "*Love one another, as I have loved you*" (John 13:34).

(Just over a year ago I was privileged to hear a message by Gaylord Ens, from California. The message, entitled "Shift", made a profound impression on me. With his indulgence, I want to pass on the gist of this message, as I have begun to do in the preceding paragraph. We need to get this!) A lawyer once asked Jesus what the greatest commandment in the law was (Matt.22:35-40). Jesus replied, "*You* shall love the LORD *your* God with all *your* heart, with all *your* soul, and with all *your* mind ... and ...*You* shall love *your* neighbor as *yourself*." Then He added, "*On these two commandments hang all the law and the prophets.*" In other words, this was the command of the old covenant, with the emphasis on YOU, and YOUR efforts; and no person on earth was able to keep it! But Jesus established a *new* covenant, and a *new* command! (Read Luke 16:16 again.) <u>The old was replaced with the new</u>! Never again did Jesus espouse those words from the old covenant; nor did the apostles. Why do we?? The theme of the new love song is *not us loving God*, but *God loving us*! Jesus came to show us the Father, and His love, so that we would know how to love one another (John 15:9, 12; 17:23). John called himself the disciple whom Jesus loved, not because He was Jesus' favorite, but he understood the Father's love, and love is the theme of his writings in the New Testament.

Take a look at these 'love' verses. John 3:16 – "God so loved ... that He gave His Son"; 1 John 4:8, 10 – "God *is* love"; "In this is love, not that we loved God, but that He loved us and sent His Son.."; Rom.5:8 – God showed us His love, in the death of Christ for us while we were still sinners; 1 John 3:1 – "what manner of love the Father has bestowed (lavished) on us, that we should be called children of God!" God pours this 'waterfall' abundance of love into our hearts by His Holy Spirit (Rom.5:5). This enables us to love our neighbors (Rom.13:8-10 – *"Love is the fulfillment of the law."*) We are empowered by God's perfect love to even love our enemies, and ourselves. As we are filled to overflowing with the love of God, it just spills out to bless others.

"We love Him because He first loved us" (1 John 4:11, 19). I will always remember the picture in my mind, as Pastor Ens described a father holding his new baby on his outstretched arm, with its head cradled in his hand. Imagine that new dad shaking his finger at the baby, and saying, "Okay, Junior. Here's the deal. I'm the boss here, and I demand that you love and obey me"! No, it doesn't work that way. A father loves his child, and tells the child over and over how much he loves him. The child naturally responds with love, and with obedience. As we know the love of *our heavenly Father* (Eph.3:17-19), we will love Him, and will be and do what He wants. Our love for Him will be heightened, not diminished. We will love God in response to His love; it's not 'performance motivated'. Loving Him is not a burden, or a work of the flesh. Eph.5:1-2 gives us another father – child picture. Just as a child imitates his father, and tries to walk in his footprints, we are to imitate

God, by walking in love as Christ loved us. In John 15:9-12, Jesus told His disciples (including us) to abide in His love, "Be at home in My love; make My love your home, the place you live in." If we obey His word (1John 1:5) we will live in His love, and in His joy. So, our joy will be complete, and we will love one another. It will flow from a heart purified by the Spirit and the Word (1Pet.1:22).

Because it is God's Spirit who fills us with His love, it is accompanied by all the gifts God has for us, everything we need to reach out in ministry to others, and everything we need for our own life and godliness (2 Pet.1:3-4). Every gift of the Spirit must be used in love (1 Cor.13), and there's a never-ending supply of this love from God.

I would encourage you to lift your love song to God as you walk along life's road with Him! But also listen to His amazing song of love, to be always reminded that we love Him only because He loved us first. Here are some of the verses in His love song: Gal.2:20; 5:22-23; Eph.2:4-7; 5:25-27; John 16:27; 17:23; 14:21, 23; 1 Cor.13; 2 Cor.5:17; 13:11; 1 Thes.3:12; 1 Pet.1:22; Rev.1:5.

And now a few 'love notes' to tuck into your backpack: God rejoices over you, quiets you with His love, and rejoices over you with singing (Zeph.3:17). Nothing can separate you from God's love (Rom.8:35-39). God has amazing blessings to pour out on those who love Him (1 Cor.2:9). Love edifies and nourishes the body of Christ (Eph.4:15-16; Phil.1:9-11; Col.2:2). God's perfect love casts out fear (1 John 4:18). "May the Lord direct your hearts into the love of God"! (2 Thes.3:5) "Above all things have fervent love for one another, for love will cover a multitude of sins" (1 Pet.4:8). AMEN! Brighten your path – keep singing your new love song! (Col.3:16)

30

PRAISE TO OUR GOD

I n our theme verse (Psa.40:3), David describes the new song as "praise to our God". In this context, praise is an act of worship, and means 'to bless, exalt, extol, magnify, laud, celebrate, adore and acclaim'. Many books could be, and have been, written about praise; so a few hundred words here can only scratch the surface of the topic. A few things need to be emphasized up front: For a redeemed and sanctified child of God, praise is essential to keeping our focus on God. It is a natural response to God's blessings of love and mercy in our lives. In order for sincere praise to come off our tongue, the heart must be pure (Isa.29:13; Jas.3:8-16). Praise includes, but is not confined to, 'church worship'; it can be expressed at any time and by many means (Psa.34:1-2; 47:1; 33:1-3; 149:3; 150:1-6).

The first occurrence of the word 'praise' in the Bible is found in Genesis 29:35. Leah had just given birth to her fourth son, and decided it was reason for praise to God. She named her son 'Judah', which means 'praise' or 'celebrate'. From the kingly line of Judah came the Messiah, Jesus. He is the One who as King of kings will receive everlasting honor and power (1 Tim.6:15-16; 1 Pet.4:11) *to the praise and glory of the Father* (Phil.2:9-11). All that Jesus is, and everything Jesus does in fulfilling God's great plan of Salvation for mankind, brings praise to God the Father (Eph.1:3-6). The following verses, 7-14 go on to say that Jesus has done all this for the purpose of calling out a family of God's children who would "be to the praise of His glory" (Isa.43:21). Just the fact that we have been redeemed, and have received His Spirit to live within us, should cause us to praise God (1 Cor.6:19-20; 1 Pet.2:9). As His children, *every moment of our lives* should be a hymn of praise in honor of Him! (1 Cor.10:31; Phil.1:9-11; Heb.13:15) If our lives are not bringing praise to God, let's get on our faces before Him, and allow His Spirit to change us into the likeness of Christ (Rom.8:29; 2 Cor.3:17-18).

It's interesting that in Strong's Concordance, over half of the references to praise are found in the Psalms, which tells me that words and music are major components of praise. Several Hebrew words are used in the Old Testament to express the meaning of praise. 'Zamar' gives the idea of striking the strings of a *musical instrument* (Psa.21:13), and these were used often in Temple worship (2 Chron.5:12-14). The word 'Yadah' expresses worshiping with *extended hands* (1 Chron.16:7). 'Tehilla' refers to a *hymn of praise* (Psa.35:28). 'Barak' simply means *blessing (Psa.72:15).* 'Halal' conveys the thought of *ridiculously loud, exuberant praise; boasting, raving and celebrating* (Psa.150). 'Shebach' means *to adulate and adore* (Dan.2:23). And 'Towdah' suggests *a choir of worshippers*, offering *a sacrifice of praise, thanksgiving, avowal and adoration* (Psa.42:4). Praise in prayer and song was expressed, not only corporately, and not only in the Temple. Many of the Psalms are individual expressions of praise to God for His holiness, faithfulness, mercy, love, and deliverance. Songs of praise were sung after a victory in war (Exod.15:1-2; Judg.5:1-3) and before battles (2 Chron.20:17-

19). Special occasions called for praise i.e. bringing back the ark to the tabernacle (1 Chron.16:1-6); finishing the building of the temple (2Chron.5:13-14); and laying the foundation of the restored temple (Ezra 3:10-11).

Why praise God? As the omnipotent, omniscient and omnipresent creator and sustainer of the universe; as the giver of life to all, and the only hope of eternal life and salvation; and as the God of love, mercy, justice and holiness, He is altogether deserving of praise (Psa.96:4-5; 145:3 – Read both of these Psalms in their entirety for a glimpse of God's worthiness). When we praise God we acknowledge that we are totally dependent on Him for absolutely everything, starting with each breath we breathe (Acts 17:28a), and we give credit where credit is due (Eph.1:3ff; 2 Pet.1:3-4). God delights in us when we praise Him (Psa.149:3-4). He is enthroned in the praises of His people – our praise releases His kingdom in our lives to manifest His blessings to us, and to move on our behalf (Psa.22:3; Matt.6:9-10). Praise reminds us of God's goodness and presence, even in the midst of worldly distractions and enemy attacks, filling us with His peace (Psa.66:1-4, 12; Phil.4:6-9). Praise enables us to see God in a deeper way (Psa.150:2; Psa.100), because in praise we are fellowshipping with Him. As we learn more of who God is, the more we will fellowship with Him in praise (Psa.48:10), and the more our entire lives will become expressions of His praise, which will be evident to all people (Psa.40:3). Praise the LORD!

Who should praise God? After Jesus rode into Jerusalem in the midst of a supportive, enthusiastic crowd, and went into the temple, some children began crying out," Hosanna to the Son of David". To the indignant Pharisees who protested this adulation, Jesus said, "if these should keep silent, the stones would immediately cry out". As a matter of fact, nature *does* praise the LORD! During creation "the morning stars sang together (Job 38:7). Psa.19 tells us "The heavens declare the glory of God". Psa.148 commands the angels and hosts of God; the sun, moon and stars, the heavens, the sea and clouds; rain, hail, snow, wind and fire; mountains, hills and trees; all creatures of the sea, earth and sky; kings, princes and judges; all people, young and old, male and female (in other words, all creation), to praise the LORD, "for His name alone is exalted" (v.13). Notice the words at the end of the psalm: "*the LORD has exalted* the horn (strength or dominion) of His people, *the praise of all His saints.* "Let everything that has breath praise the LORD" (Psa.150:6). "Praise the LORD, all you Gentiles! Laud Him, all you peoples" (Psa.17:1). "Sing praise to the LORD, you saints of His, and give thanks at the remembrance of His holy name" (Psa.30:4). God acknowledges praise from all of His creation, but to His ears, the sweetest of all are the praises of His chosen ones, those who know Him and love Him from their heart, those who know His language of love, and express their praise with songs of joy (Eph.5:19-20).

Throughout the Old Testament, God revealed himself to people with a special revelation of His NAME. When we praise the NAME of God we include the attributes connected with that name. Specifically, we can praise Him for each of His individual attributes. i.e. Dan.2:20 – wisdom and might; 2 Chron.20:21 – mercy; Isa.25:1 – truth, faithfulness, and wonderful deeds; Psa.138:2, 5 – loving-kindness and glory; Exod.15:11 – holiness; Isa.24:14 – majesty; Luke 1:68-69 – redemption; Psa.107:8 – goodness; Psa.21:13 – power; Psa.145:3 – greatness. See Col.1:12-14; Eph.1:3-14; 2:4-8; 3:16-21. Determine today to praise Him yet more and more! (Psa.71:14) It's good for you!!

31

SONGS OF JOY AND PEACE

𝕊𝕖

J oy and peace – to me they belong together, and like the old song says, "You can't have one without the other"! They are side by side in the fruit-bowl of Gal.5:22-23, and at the top of the list of Love's components. We find them hand in hand in Rom.14:17 and 15:13; and connected by prayer in vs.2 and 4 of Paul's salutation to the church in Philippi. In Phil.4:4, 7, they are close neighbors; in vs.9-10 only six small words separate them. When we have the fullness of the *joy of the Lord* alongside the deep, settled, inexplicable *peace of God*, made possible by *peace with God,* we will have the ability to sing, and beautiful themes for our song. Joy and peace are both special gifts from our Savior (John 15:11; 17:13; 14:27; 16:33; Luke 1:79), bequeathed to His church just before His death on the cross to wrap up the whole amazing Salvation gift with a scarlet cord. Do you realize what absolutely wonderful gifts joy and peace are? We keep them in our heart and mind, and yet wear them on our face - obvious when present, and conspicuous by their absence. There are no substitutes – only the genuine goods can produce a contented spirit as well as a joyful, peaceful countenance, like the 'song of praise' that people will see, and be drawn to the Lord (Psa. 40:3). Gal.5:22 indicates that joy and peace come along with the gift of the Holy Spirit, so if the Holy Spirit is not received, welcomed and treasured in our life, but is quenched and grieved by our rejection and unbelief, we are in fact refusing the joy and peace provided for us in Jesus' will. Something to think about!

The whole world is in a relentless pursuit of happiness. I use the word 'happiness', because to most people, the word 'joy' is not in their vocabulary, or it is given a very superficial meaning. Happiness is based on 'happenings' or outward circumstances, so it can come or go, continually fluctuating. The joy from the Lord is planted within us, and is constant in spite of things that come at us in life (1 Pet.4:12-13). Happiness is elusive, and is almost always just beyond our reach. The words, "I'd be happy if only ..." mock us, and happiness slips from our grasp, as we reach for the next thing that we hope will make us happy. We expect things, pleasures or people to give us happiness, and are usually disappointed, because they can't satisfy (Eccl.2:10-11). "The joy of the Lord is (our) strength" (Neh.8:10), bearing us up through hard times, because God is the source of our joy, and He does not let us down (Jude 24). All through the Bible the word 'joy' is linked with God's presence, favor and blessing (Psa.16:11). Joy is present in worship (1 Chron.15:16; 29:9), on Feast days (2 Chron.30:21, 26) and in times of war (2 Chron.20:27; Psa.5:11-12). Joy flows out of a pure heart (Psa.32:11), and God is our joy in the midst of oppression (Psa.43:2-4; Luke 6:22-23; Jas.1:2). Joy is abundant in God's salvation (Isa.12:2-3; 35:10; Hab.3:17-18), in a humble heart (Isa.29:19) and in God's word (Jer.15:16). Jesus' birth was announced as tidings of great joy (Luke 2:10) because of the good news of the Gospel He would usher in (Acts 8:5-8; Rom.5:11). Jesus gives us joy in place of tears (Isa.61:1-3), and He promised that no one will take our joy from us (John 16:22). He also assured us that our joy will be full, when in

Jesus' name we ask for and receive from the Father what we need (John 16:23-24). Dear friend, "Rejoice with joy inexpressible and full of glory" in believing (1 Pet.1:8).

In the same way that the *joy of the Lord* sustains us in the storm, so the *peace of God* reigns in our heart and mind (Col.3:15) even when our world is crashing around us. That is because it is not the world's peace; it is not a peace due to the *absence* of conflict, but peace in the *midst* of conflict, a heart untroubled and free from fear (John 14:27). "It is well with my soul" – a perfect well-being, "whatever my lot"! Peace could be considered an antonym for fear; they are unable to exist together. Two of the most recorded short commands of Jesus to his disciples are "Fear not / Do not be afraid" (Matt.10:31; 14:27; 28:10; Mark 5:36; Luke 1:13, 30; 5:10; 12:7; John 6:20; 14:27) and "Peace be unto you" (Luke 24:36; John 20:19, 21, 26). His desire was that their hearts and minds be rid of fear, and infused with His peace (Phil.4:6-7). The peace theme also appears in the salutations of the apostolic letters to the churches, and sometimes in their closing words, often in tandem with grace, and mercy, because peace is the *birthright of every believer* (1 Pet.5:14). Colossians 1:20 tells us that we are reconciled to God, at peace with Him through the blood of the cross. Romans 5:1 says that because we have been justified by faith through the Lord Jesus Christ, we have peace with God. In Romans 8:6, he teaches that being spiritually minded is life and peace. Peace should be the way of life for every believer.

In addition to the pearls of peace already mentioned, I want to focus on the varied aspects of this restful word. Romans and Ephesians both talk about *"the gospel of peace"*. In writing about how the Jewish people rejected the gospel, and yet those who believed have become part of the church composed of both Jew and Gentile, Paul wrote, "How beautiful are the feet of those who preach the gospel of peace" – Rom.10:15. It is the gospel of peace because it broke down the wall of partition between Jew and Gentile, and made them one in Christ. In Eph.2:14-22, speaking to this, Paul says that *Jesus "Himself is our peace"*, who through the cross destroyed the enmity and established peace. He came and preached peace to both Jew and Gentile (v.17). Eph.6:15 says our feet are to be shod "with the preparation of the gospel of peace." According to Eph.4:3, *peace* is the anointing that *keeps us one in the unity of the Spirit*. Paul re-emphasizes this in 2 Cor.13:11: "be of one mind, live in peace". Peter, in talking of the frightening signs accompanying the Day of the Lord, tells us to "be diligent to *be found by Him in peace*, without spot and blameless" (2 Pet.3:14). See another golden nugget in Jas.3:17-18.

There are several references in the epistles to *the God of peace*:

- Heb.13:20-21 - The God of peace who raised Jesus from the dead, works in us to make us complete and well-pleasing to Him, enabling us (by His resurrection power through the Spirit) to do His will in every good work.
- 1 Thes.5:23 – The God of peace wants to sanctify us completely, and to preserve us blameless - body, soul and spirit - at the coming of our Lord Jesus Christ.
- Phil.4:9b – "The God of peace will be with you". That is wonderfully comforting!
- Rom.16:20 – "The God of peace (not of war) will crush Satan under your feet shortly." YES!

"Go out with joy, and be led forth with peace" (Isa.55:12; Rom.15:13; 14:17) SHALOM!

32

THE WILL OF GOD

*W*hat is more preached on, prayed about, agonized over
or sought after in Christian circles than 'the will of
God'? It seems to me, from observation and personal experience, that the way we often define it is different from the teaching
in the scriptures. It's as though we have the em-pha'-sis on the
wrong syl-la'-ble! As a result, when we get older, we often look
back on our life with regrets, because we took the wrong road;
we wasted so many years; we failed as a Christian... We may
feel (wrongly so) that if we are not serving God in some 'spiritual' role, such as a pastor, evangelist or missionary, that we are
not fulfilling His purpose for us, that somehow we are of less
value in God's economy. Where did *that* idea come from? It
may seem strange to even broach the subject of the will of God
at this point in our journey, but being in and doing the will of
God is what we were made for, so what better time to talk about
it? We've been redeemed from the slavery of sin, (yet wandered in the wilderness for years perhaps, hoping we'll reach
that land of plenty some day). But now, at last, by God's grace,
we've been brought out of the horrible pit of fears of the future
and hurts from the past. Our feet have been freed from the miry
clay of self-righteousness, self-condemnation, and self-pity,
etc. God has been with us through the battles, as many enemies

of our mind and heart have been vanquished. He has even put a new song in our mouth, and we're resting in the peace and joy He promised. We're walking with Him on His highway, getting to know Him, learning His ways, and taking possession of more and more of all His blessings. We have come to the place where we not only desire, out of a pure heart, to do the will of God, but to the place of sanctification where God can actually use us, where we will bring glory to Him with our restored life!

We see as we look at the 'famous' people in the Bible, that they were *ordinary people*, going about their daily routines, when God stepped into their lives, and called them to a special job i.e. Moses – Exod.3:1, 6, 10; Gideon – Judg.6:11-12, 15-16; David – 1 Sam.16:11-12; Elisha – 1 Kings 19:19; Jeremiah – Jer.1:1, 4-10; Peter – Matt.4:18-20; Paul – Acts 26:9-18. In each case, *God made His plan for them abundantly clear*. I really don't think He chose them because they were gifted, but *He gifted them for the task*. They had not applied for the job; they weren't even looking for His will! But *God chose them* - the weak, the insignificant, and the unlikely, to further His kingdom, and bring glory to His name. They had no preconceived ideas of what God might want them to do, they had not done any aptitude tests, or taken any specific training, and they weren't sitting around waiting for 'the call'. They were *just being faithful* in the normal 'making a living' daily work. What is important, when God called, *they responded*, albeit sometimes reluctantly. And, *they were willing to leave* their means of livelihood, their home and family, their friends and their possessions; *they were ready to suffer*, even to death, for the One who called them. Not many people are chosen to be a Gideon or a Paul. Do not aspire to be great in God's kingdom. If you are serving with humility and faithfulness where you are, you are in the right place for God's promotion (Jas.4:10).

Maybe we are neglecting God's calling for *all* His people, while in search of His calling for '*me*', specifically. What, exactly, is God's calling for our lives? Are you ready? We are CALLED: out of darkness, and the power of darkness into light – a new King and a new kingdom (1 Pet.2:9; Col.1:13); to be saints, that is set apart to God, pure, holy (Rom.1:7; 1 Cor.1:2; 1 Thes.4:7; 1 Pet.1:15); to liberty i.e. freedom from sin and religious bondage (Rom.8:2; 2 Cor.3:17; Gal.5:1, 13); to partake of His glory (Rom.8:28-30; 2 Thes.2:14 - this is for now, not just the future – 2 Cor.3:18); to eternal life (1 Tim.6:12; 2 Pet.1:10-11 – We have this life *now*, the divine eternal life of Christ in us – Col.1:27); to an inheritance in the future (1 Pet.1:4; Heb.9:15; Rom.8:17; Eph.1:11-14; Col.1:12); to love – a perfect love that casts out fear (1 John 4:17-18; 1 Pet.3:8-9; John 13:34); to be the bride of Christ – glorious, holy and without blemish (Eph.5:25-27; Rev.19:6-9). We are also called to be blameless, harmless, and without fault (1 Thes.5:23; Phil.2:15); to be His witnesses and ambassadors here on earth (Acts 1:8; 2 Cor.5:20); to be kings and priests of God to reign with Christ for a thousand years (1 Pet.2:9; Rev.1:5-6; 5:9-10; 20:6). We are called children / sons of God (1 John 3:1; John 1:12). Every child of God has been called to these things. Let us walk worthy of our calling! (Eph.4:1-3)

GOD'S WILL for your life, and for mine, will fit within these guidelines of our calling. Contrary to what we might think, God has a lot to say in His word about what His will is for us. He *does want us to know His will* (Col.1:9). He *wants His will to be done in us* and through us here on earth, as it is done in heaven (Matt.6:10; Heb.13:20-21). He promises that *He will enable us to do His will* - the good works He wants us to do, Himself doing the work in us (Heb.13:21; Eph.2:10; Phil.1:6; 2:12-13; 2 Thes.2:16-17). THIS is God's will for you: to "rejoice always, pray without ceasing, in everything give thanks (1 Thes.5:16-18); to "present your bodies a living sacrifice ... to God" and "be transformed by the renewing of your mind" (Rom.12:1-2); to please Him, and have fruitful lives of good works, filled with His power, wisdom and joyful patience (Col.1:9-11); "your sanctification: that you should abstain from sexual immorality" (1 Thes.4:3); to trust God, and not be anxious about tomorrow (Matt.6:25-34); to silence foolish thinking by doing good (1 Pet.3:15); to seek *His* kingdom, not build our own (Matt.6:19-21); to be filled with His Spirit and know His love (Eph.3:16-19).

I believe that as we are faithful in obedience to what he has told us, He will guide us into the specifics for our lives. Before revelation must come a hunger for God Himself, obedience and faithfulness in what we already know of His will, and surrender to the Holy Spirit in every area of our lives, so that when He tells us to do something, we know His voice, we listen and we obey, no matter how insignificant or strange it may seem. This is the message of Romans 12:1-2, which we quote so glibly sometimes. In essence Paul is saying here that we will not know and be able to do God's perfect will for us unless and until: 1) we are *completely surrendered to Him*; 2) we have cast off the works of *this world's darkness* i.e. been sanctified (1 John 2:15-16; Col.3:5-9); and 3) *our minds have been renewed* by the Holy Spirit and the Word (Tit.3:5-6; Phil.2:5; Col.3:1-4; 10-17). God does not force His will on us. The first step in knowing His will is yielding *our* will to His. **If we want *God's will* in our life, we have to give up *our will*** – it's absolutely the only way and the best choice! Rejoice in His will! Be assured that God wants to guide you, but He will do so only if we let Him! (Prov.3:5-6; Psa.32:8)

33

LAW AND WORKS
or GRACE AND FAITH

ℒℯ

*T*he Apostle Paul describes his life prior to faith in Christ as "a Hebrew of the Hebrews ... a Pharisee ... concerning the righteousness which is in the law, blameless" (Phil.3:4-6; Acts 22:3; 26:5). After his blinding encounter with Jesus on the Damascus road, God told Ananias concerning him: "he is a chosen vessel of Mine to bear My name before Gentiles, kings, and the children of Israel" (Acts 9:15). Within days of this calling Paul began to preach Christ as the Son of God and Messiah to his fellow Jews (Acts 9:20-22). To Paul the calling was irrevocable, and his passion to carry out this mandate was stirred to the depth of his being. But God had to rein Paul in for a while. You see, Paul was steeped in the teaching of the old covenant. He was taught by the best rabbi in all of Israel that his righteousness before God depended on him keeping the law, not just the Ten Commandments, but every ordinance and rule contained in the Torah, including offering animal sacrifices. Suddenly, he was called to follow Jesus Christ, who had come to establish a new covenant. He was called to be a special minister of this new covenant (2 Cor.3:5-6), but what did he know

154

about it? He had not lived under the teaching of Jesus, as had the twelve disciples. Even as he had probably read about the Messiah and the new covenant in the prophetic writings (Isa.42 and 53; Jer.31:31; Mal.3:1), his eyes were veiled from the truth, to which he later testifies (2 Cor.3:14-16). God put Paul's ministry on hold, apparently for several years of debriefing and re-teaching by His new instructor, the Holy Spirit (Gal.1:17-18; 2:1). During this time he was taken to heaven and received inexpressible revelations and saw indescribable visions (2 Cor.12:1-4). As a result, Paul's entire theological belief system was turned upside down (Phil.3:7-10). No longer did he depend on his own good works in an effort to gain righteousness before God, but on his faith in Christ, through God's gift of salvation. He had crossed over from law to grace! (Gal.2:15-21)

The theme of salvation by grace through faith, as opposed to the works of the law, shines through in all of Paul's teaching. Beginning with his proclamation in Rom.1:16, he goes on to argue for it and expound on it for the first eight chapters of the book, with intermittent references to it throughout the other eight chapters. To highlight just a few texts from his other letters, see 2 Cor.3:5-18; Gal.1-5; Eph.2:8-9; Phil.3:3-9; Col.2:11-23; 1 Tim.1:3-9; 2 Tim.1:9; Tit.3:5-7. Also see Acts 13:38-39; 15:6-11. The book of Hebrews deals almost exclusively with the shift from the old covenant to the new, better covenant. It seems that many of the believing Jews of Paul's day found it hard to get into the mindset of the new covenant of grace and faith, wanting to cling to tradition and the outward signs of the Jewish religion they had grown up with. Some of them even tried to impose these outward ordinances on the Gentile believers (hence the reason for the writing of his letter to the Galatians). So what has this to do with us today? Over the years and centuries, the same type of works-and-tradition-teaching that Paul fought against, has crept in, ever so subtly, to erode and corrupt the grace-faith freedom in Christ that he guarded so fervently. If he were here today, he would likely ask us, as he did the Galatians, "Who has bewitched you? Are you so foolish? Having begun in the Spirit, are you now made perfect by the flesh?" (Gal.3:1, 3)

It's still the same issue. We know that we are born into the family of God through the new birth by the Holy Spirit, as we accept by faith Christ's death on the cross for our sin. But, like the Galatians, this same Holy Spirit who wants to empower us; to be our comforter, helper, guide and teacher; to fill us with His love, joy, peace and hope; to baptize us and give us special gifts for ministry, has been ignored and forgotten by so much of the church today. In His place, we have gone about to try and produce all the right fruit and all the right works by making up rules and rituals to follow, and regimented good works to keep us busy. (These often fall under the title of 'disciplines', a term based on the word 'disciple'). Thus have we unwittingly, and with all good intention put ourselves and our 'disciples' under bondage to legalism. Our Christian walk has often been full of striving, condemnation, guilt and despair, because in our own strength we simply don't measure up, and we can't overcome the works of the sin nature within us. The New Testament does talk about good works – not the works we do to try and keep God happy, but the works *He wants to do in us* through the power of the Spirit! The first thing we need to do is repent of the dead works of fleshly effort (Heb.6:1), break off the shackles of religious legalism, and begin to walk in the freedom of the Spirit (Gal.5:1; 2 Cor.3:17).

Let's travel back to the time when Jesus called twelve men to follow Him, men who would later be known as His disciples. Every day for three years, these men witnessed a man who was baptized in God's Spirit (Matt.3:16-17) live a pure, holy, joyful, peaceful and loving life, and then accept death on the cross so that they could be like Him! They saw Him live in close fellowship with, and obedience to, the Father, and use the power of the Holy Spirit within Him to heal the sick and cast out demons (Luke 4:33-41). They saw His compassion for people, and His desire to bring lost sheep into His fold. They heard Him teach principles of the Kingdom, and saw how He lived them out. By word and action He showed them the Father's love for Him, and for them. I venture to say they learned more about being a disciple from what they saw, than from what they heard (1 John 1:1-3).

So when Jesus left them with the mandate to go and make disciples (His, not theirs), they knew they needed the same power in them that Jesus had, and they waited in prayer for the Holy Spirit baptism (Luke 24:49; Acts 2:1-4). They had learned well from the Master, and "preached repentance and remission of sins in His name to all nations" (Luke 24:47; Acts2:11b). On the first day, three thousand people responded to their message! As directed, they baptized those who repented (Matt.28:19; Acts 2:41), ensuring that they understood the importance of receiving the baptism of the Holy Spirit (Acts 2:38-39; 8:14-17; 10:44-48; 19:1-6). They, like their mentor, by the power of the Holy Spirit, healed the sick (Acts 3:1-10; Acts 5:15-16), cast out evil spirits (v.16) and raised the dead (Acts 9:36-42). Signs and wonders followed them and the new 'disciples' (Mark 16:17-18; Acts 6:8; 8:5-7). These people learned from Jesus, imitated Him, and taught His words to others. And they walked in the freedom and power of the Holy Spirit, unshackled by the traditions of men. They knew that "where the Spirit of the Lord is, there is liberty". They depended on *Him* to teach, guide and empower them and to change them into the image of Christ (2 Cor.3:17-18). May we do likewise, and experience true freedom!

34

ASK AND RECEIVE

૭

W e may have listened to someone pray, and thought, "I'll never be able to pray like that! They have all the right words, and sound so holy. Surely God will answer that prayer!" There are a few great prayers of gratitude and petition in the scriptures, such as David's (2 Sam.7:18-29; and Solomon's (1 Kings 8:22-53); and the relatively short prayers of Paul for the church in Eph.1:15-23; 3:14-21; Phil.1:9-11; and Col.1:9-14. But many times, the prayers of the patriarchs, prophets, priests, kings and apostles are not recorded. When a 'situation' arises, we often read words such as "and Moses prayed", or "Elisha prayed", or "prayer was made". Even though the Gospels tell us that Jesus spent many hours and nights in prayer, few of His prayers are recorded; those that are, with the exception of His prayer on the night of His betrayal (John 17), are short, simple and from the heart (Luke 22:32; John 11:41-42; Matt.26:39; 27:46). Jesus warned against praying like the Pharisees, who stood in the synagogues and on street corners for show; and like the heathen, using 'vain repetitions', and 'many words' (Matt.6:5-7). It was the publican's seven-word cry for mercy, from a contrite heart that reached God's ear, and was answered; not the boastful prayer of the Pharisee (Luke 18:10-14). I would suggest that it's *not eloquence or abundance of words* that is important in prayer, and we should not make this our goal. What counts is *a pure and contrite heart* (Psa.7:10; 15:1-2; 51:10, 17; 66:18; 73:1; 139:23-24), and clean lips (Psa.17:1; Psa.19:12-14; Isa.6:5-7; Jas.3:10).

Rather than try to define prayer, let's look at what might be involved in prayer, focusing on what prayer means to a believer in Christ. It was after witnessing Jesus at prayer that His disciples asked Him to teach them to pray (*not how to pray*, but to *pray* – it is more important that we spend time with the Father in prayer, than making sure we get the words right, or use the right posture or tone of voice!). The prayer that Jesus taught His disciples (Matt.6:9-13) is not the only way to pray, but it gives us a pattern and some important components of prayer. First, it is *God the Father* we are to address, *our* Father *in heaven*, not an earthly or religious 'father'. We are to acknowledge the holiness of His Name, praying *with reverence*. We are to pray for *God's will to be done* on earth (in me, in His people (the church), in governments and nations, etc.) We look to God *for daily needs* (not take them for granted). We *ask for His forgiveness*, where we have come short, and agree that we must *forgive those who wrong us* (See Mark 11:25-26). We ask Him to *keep us on His path*, and protect us from *our enemy*, Satan. And, we *offer Him the praise* due to Him. Jesus later told His disciples: "If you *abide in Me*, and *My words abide in you*, you will ask what you desire, and it shall be done for you" (John 15:7). It is as we spend time with Jesus, delighting in Him, and in His Word, that *our desires become what He wants for us* (Psa.37:4-5). That is why He can say to His close friends: "Whatever you *ask the Father in My name*, He will give you ... Ask, and you will receive, that your joy may be full" (John 16:23-24). Heb.4:14-16 and 7:24-25 show us that *Jesus is our great High Priest*, who stands before the Father to intercede for us; hence we are to come to God through Jesus, i.e. in His name. It is through Jesus' sacrifice for us that we can ask the Father for what we need.

Prayer is not only prominent in the lives of people under the old covenant, and in the life of Jesus, but very much evident in the lives and writings of the Apostles and others in the early church. By looking at some of their references to prayer, we can get a better understanding of prayer, and its importance in our lives. Here are a few things to note. Firstly, there is no prescribed prayer posture. Thankfully, for those confined to their beds, we don't need to stand with arms upraised, bow our heads, kneel, or lie prostrate on our faces. It's not the body's position, but the heart's condition that counts. Secondly, there is no one method of prayer we must use. We are told rather to pray with all / 'all kinds of' prayer (Eph.6:18). Thirdly, there is no time restriction placed on prayer. Surprisingly, we are told to "continue *steadfastly* in prayer" (Rom.12:12; Col.4:2; Acts 6:4), *"pray always"* (Eph.6:18; 2 Thes.1:11; Col.1:3), *"without ceasing"* (1 Thes.5:17; Col.1:9). If we can't do this, perhaps we have the wrong concept of prayer. Actually prayer is spending time with God, and God's Spirit dwells in our spirit. At any given time, sleeping or awake, He can commune with us in our spirit, and our spirit can commune with Him i.e. *"Praying always* with all prayer and supplication *in the Spirit"* (Eph.6:18). When we are conscious, our minds can communicate with Him, with or without words. Paul says in 1 Cor.14:14-15, "If I pray *in a tongue*, my spirit prays, but my understanding is unfruitful … I will pray *with the spirit*, and I will pray *with the understanding"*. Also see Jude 20 and Rom.8:26-27. Praying in the Spirit is being continuously in God's presence, sometimes receiving revelations of His truth, or just enjoying the peace, joy and love of His presence. At other times we may be in intercession or supplication for the saints as the Spirit brings them to our mind. We may be asking for something we need, or praising and giving God thanks for all His wonderful blessings. We can be in prayer in the midst of our busy days, and in the inactivity of sleep, by praying in the Spirit.

Here are some more directives in the Word, about praying. "Let us come *boldly* to the throne of grace, that we may obtain mercy and find grace to help *in time of need*" (Heb.4:16). We do not need to tremble in God's presence, because through Christ, His throne is not one of judgment, but of abundant grace and mercy for us. He wants us to go to Him for help when we are needy, rather than struggling on our own, or seeking help from the world. We are also to *persevere in prayer* (Eph.6:18), not growing weary or giving up when the answer seems slow in coming. James reiterates this and adds that we need to *ask in faith*, not doubting (Jas.1:5-8). Also see Mark 11:22-24. In Phil.4:6 Paul tells us: "*In everything* by prayer and supplication, with thanksgiving, *let your requests be made known to God*" According to this verse, there is really nothing we should not pray about, but we are especially to pray instead of being anxious about anything. At the same time, we are to *give thanks* as we pray. Another thing, even though God already knows what we need, he wants us to ask Him – in fact He delights in hearing the requests of His children, and providing them with all they need and more (Jer.29:11). And, as James tells us, the prayers of a righteous person are *effective, fervent and successful* (Jas.5:14-16), and are to be exercised in the church for *the ministry of healing*. But prayer is powerful only in the sense that it is infused and endued with the Holy Spirit's power. It is God who is powerful, not prayer in and of itself. Prayer is a privilege. Ask and receive! (Luke 11:9-13)

35

SINGING IN THE RAIN

❧

*W*ho *sings* in the *rain*?? Well, Gene Kelley, for one, and maybe some robins (in anticipation of the juicy earthworms that surface from the wet soil). Where I live, and also where I grew up, there are many thunder and lightning storms throughout the summer, often with strong winds, heavy rain or pelting hail. I've noticed that people react in three different ways to these onslaughts of nature. Some run for cover, hide under the bed, and cover their eyes and ears. Others (myself included) make sure that 'all the hatches are battened down', and then carry on with life as usual. A third group embraces the storm, enthralled by the wonder of the thunder, the beauty of the lightning and the force of the wind and rain / hail. Of course, in the wake of hurricanes, tornados and tsunamis, none of these reactions is an option – even if you are warned and protected, you may still suffer huge loss, or become 'a statistic'.

It would be remiss of me to convey the idea that the pilgrim journey we are on with God is all warmth and sunshine. Life happens, as they say. And for a person who is yielded to God, committed to living life in the Spirit and following Jesus, storms also come in the form of opposition and persecution, instigated by that evil enemy of our souls, to test our faith (Jas.1:2-3; 1 Pet.1:6-7; 4:12). Many of us in the western world cannot imagine the extent to which believers in some countries are tortured and killed for their refusal to renounce Jesus. It's been going on against God's people for centuries (Heb.11:32-38 and 'Fox's Book of Martyrs'). Satan's ongoing vendetta against genuine, Spirit-filled believers is real, and his attacks are relentless and vicious. But, like the house built on the rock, we can withstand the storms that come from whatever source, if we are firmly established on the Rock of our salvation, hearing and doing His sayings (Matt.7:24-25). Remember the words of Shadrach, Meshach and Abednego as they faced death by fire, for refusing to bow to an image of gold? "Our God whom we serve is able to deliver us from the burning fiery furnace, and He will deliver us from your hand, O king. But if not ... we do not serve your gods, nor will we worship the gold image which you have set up" (Dan.3). These young men knew their God! Another young man stood before the formidable Goliath, and said, "The LORD does not save with sword and spear; for the battle is the LORD's, and He will give you into our hands" (1 Sam.17). This same young man repeatedly praised God, his Rock and Savior, in the psalms he wrote. i.e. Psa.62:2, 6. The song in his heart kept him strong in the fight.

I think of Paul and Silas, their feet in the stocks, in a cold, filthy dungeon, praying and singing hymns to God in the middle of the night. They did not know there would be an earthquake to free them, or that the jailor and his family would believe as a result, but they faced whatever might lie ahead of them with a song of praise to the God they knew was sufficient for every storm. As the stones were hurled at Stephen, he prayed: "Lord, do not charge them with this sin" (Acts 7:60). The Christ he knew was with him even as he faced certain death (Acts 7:55-56). In 2 Cor.11:23-27 Paul writes about some of the trials and persecution he faced during his life of proclaiming the Gospel (definitely not an enviable list); and adds, "I take pleasure in infirmities, in reproaches, in needs, in persecutions, and in distresses, for Christ's sake." (2 Cor.12:10). What a testimony to God's sufficient grace! Jesus had told His followers that persecution would come (John 15:18-21); but He also promised peace and joy in the midst of our tribulation, because He has overcome the world (Matt.5:10-12; John 16:33). Paul expounds on this in Rom.8:33-39 – "We are more than conquerors through Him who loved us"! As Christ's followers, it is a privilege to suffer for His name (Acts 5:40-42; 1 Pet.4:12-16, 19). And for those who persevere through trials (Rev.12:10-11) there are special rewards! (Jas.1:2-4, 12; Rev.2:10) It *is* possible, by God's grace, to sing in the rain!

I want to address the fact that there are things we may allow in to our lives, which silence the song that even the storms of persecution cannot touch. If Satan cannot stifle our witness through death or imprisonment, he will use one of his age-old tactics. That old serpent, the devil, who tempted Eve in the Garden of Eden, and later tempted our Lord in the wilderness of Judea, is the same one who tempts us to sin and to disobey God today. He still tries to make sin attractive, to draw us away from the truth of God. Let's be clear in the fact that God does not ever tempt us to sin (Jas.1:13). The next two verses (14-15) show that temptation in itself is not a sin, but it can lead to sin. Whether or not it does is up to us. Both Eve and Jesus were tempted; Eve sinned; Jesus did not. Since temptation comes to us as a thought that is not of God, we can take the thought captive to the obedience of Christ (2 Cor.10:5) i.e. cast it out immediately in Jesus' name. This nips it in the bud. But, if we choose rather to listen to the thought, we are letting our fleshly desires draw our minds to it, and the idea begins to entice us – it starts to look good to us; and as our desire yields to the temptation, sin is conceived within the desire, and before long, sin is birthed and alive in us. *We become captive to sin when we do not take the temptation captive* (1 Cor.10:12-13). Effectively, the enemy of the sheep has stolen our song, killed our joy and destroyed our peace (John 10:10). As a result, our light is dimmed, and our testimony diminished. "Resist the devil and he will flee from you" (Jas.4:7). Don't let him take *your* song!

The issue of spiritual warfare is a recurring theme in this book, and justifiably so – Rev.12:13-17! The enraged dragon is on the warpath. He takes advantage of our hurts, our raw emotions, our circumstances, etc., to fill our mind with his lies, and he uses other people to sling his darts at us. One thing that he uses to get to us is un-forgiveness or bitterness that we may be harboring against *anyone* (2 Cor.2:10-11; Heb.12:15). He gets us to curse those who hurt us, instead of loving and blessing them and praying for them as Jesus taught us to do (Matt.5:44). Another is the sin of grumbling, complaining and fault-finding. Unless we know how to resist and rout the enemy (1 Pet.5:8-9), our whole being - body, soul and spirit will suffer. But *we can overcome* him by the blood of the Lamb, and the Word of our testimony (Rev.12:11). We can thwart his attacks of doubt, discouragement and disease by worshiping in God's presence. We can pull down all his strongholds with the mighty weapons of our warfare, "strong in the Lord and in the power of His might" (2 Cor.10:4-5; Eph.6:10-18), and confident in the authority we have in Jesus' name to cast him out (Matt.10:8). The enemy flees at the name of Jesus. So be encouraged, my fellow pilgrims! With the songs of Jesus on our lips, the enemy has no power against us (Isa.54:17). Keep singing songs in the night, and in the rain!

36

A VICTORY ANTHEM

*A*s I write, the 2012 Summer Olympics is in full swing in London, and though I haven't watched the medal ceremonies closely, in my mind I can hear the national anthems of the various countries being played and sung with pride in honor of the one person or team that was victorious over all the other contestants. Paul must have had something similar in mind when he wrote the words in 1 Cor.9:24-27. He talks about the competitors living a temperate life-style, without excesses; of disciplining their body, so it will do what the mind is telling it to do, in order that they won't be disqualified; about those who don't run with uncertainty; and boxers who aren't just beating the air. And in v.24 he writes: "Do you not know that those who run in a race all run, but one receives the prize? Run in such a way that you may obtain it." (Also see Acts 20:24). At the end of his life, this same man wrote: "I have fought the good fight, I have finished the race, I have kept the faith ... (So) there is laid up for me the crown" (2 Tim.4:7-8). Can you see him kneeling on the heavenly podium, head bowed, receiving that well-earned crown, the emblem of victory? And then, from the lips of people from every century since Christ's death, and from every tribe and nation, will rise the great swelling anthem of heaven, in praise, not to the one on the podium, but to the One who was Victor over sin, death and hell; the One who met Saul on the Damascus Road, and transformed him into Paul, "a chosen vessel ... to bear (His) name before Gentiles, kings and the children of Israel" (Acts 9:15). And Paul will cast His crown at the feet of Him who is "worthy to receive glory and honor and power" (Rev.4:10-11).

It's wonderful to contemplate the wonders and joys of heaven, but we don't have to wait for glory to sing the victor's song. Let's add the Victory Anthem to the repertoire of songs He has put in our mouth for the journey home! In regards to our victory as God's children we need to know that *God fights the battle*, wins the war, and **hands us the victory**! This is true of the physical battles in the Old Testament, and in the spiritual warfare of the church today. Think of the deliverance of the children of Israel from Egypt: From the very first plague to the Red Sea interment of Pharaoh's army, not a sword was raised by God's people; only Moses' staff was raised in faith, in obedience to God's command (Exod.7:19; 9:23; 10:13; 14:26). The LORD won the victory as they stood still and watched (Exod.14:13-14; 30-31); and they sang their victory song in praise to Him! (Exod.15: 1-21) At the edge of Canaan, Caleb and Joshua knew God would give them the land and urged the people not to fear the giants (Num.13:30; 14:6-9), but they rebelled, and died in the desert. Forty years later, Joshua led the next generation into Canaan to face their first walled city. When the priests blew trumpets and the people shouted, at God's orders, the walls of Jericho fell flat (Josh.6:5, 20). Their first conquest in Canaan was made, but not by the might of man! It was as God had promised! (Deut.1:30) Later, when Joshua and his men faced the armies of five kingdoms, God gave them a miraculous victory – read about it in Josh.10:8-14! Gideon, and three hundred men armed with torches and trumpets, went against the hordes of Midian and watched the enemy self- destruct! (Judg.7:19-22) And read about God's amazing victory on Hezekiah's behalf, while he slept! (2 Kings18:13-19:35)

Sometimes it's helpful to look back into the history of Israel in order to understand the vital truths for the church. Not only has the victory been *promised* for the church – it has been WON! In his letter to the church at Rome, Paul ends a dismal chapter of his own struggle and failure with a victory cry (Rom.7:24-25), and goes on in chapter 8 to show that through Christ, and by walking in His Spirit, we have been <u>delivered from the power of sin and death</u> (vs.2-3), and that "we <u>are more than conquerors</u> through Him who loved us" (vs.31-39). In his marvelous teaching in 1 Cor.15 on the resurrection of Christ, the "firstfruits" of the resurrection of believers at His second coming, he quotes from Isa.25:8 and Hosea 13:14: "Death is swallowed up in victory." "O Death, where is your sting? O Hades, where is your victory?" (v.54b-55) He continues "Thanks be to <u>God</u>, who <u>gives us the victory</u> through our Lord Jesus Christ"! (v.57) In 2 Cor.2:14 he exclaims "Thanks be to <u>God</u> who always <u>leads us in triumph</u> in Christ". In John's revelation, he saw the One on a white horse going out "conquering and to conquer" (Rev.6:2).

Before he went to the cross, Jesus told His disciples "I have <u>overcome the world</u>" (John 16:33). In His mind it was a done deal – it was God's plan from the beginning – He had come to carry it out through His death and resurrection. Early on in His ministry Jesus defeated Satan with the Word of God (Matt.4:10-11). Later, when Jesus was accused of casting out demons in cahoots with Satan, He taught in a parable that Satan was like a fully armed strong man, guarding his castle and his goods (plundered from his victims?). But One who is stronger than he (i.e. Jesus Christ) will come upon and <u>overcome Satan</u>, destroy his armor, and recover the spoils of his battles (Luke 11:21-22). Incidentally he also told His disciples that He cast out demons with the finger of God (v.20). John remembered His Master's words, writing in 1 John 4:1-4: "You are of God, little children, and have <u>overcome</u> them (<u>evil spirits</u> of the Antichrist), because He who is in you is greater than he who is in the world." In 1 John 2:13-14 he wrote that the recipients of his letter had overcome the wicked one, because of the One who was in them. Also in 1 John 5:4-5 he says that those born of God (who believe that Jesus is the Son of God) overcome the world. Also see Rev.12:10-11. We are told in Rom.12:21 to <u>overcome evil</u> with good. We overcome only in the power of the One who has already overcome, whose Spirit lives in us 'earthen vessels' (2 Cor.4:6-7). When we fight the battle without the power of His name, His blood and his Spirit, we lose every time!

We are to put on our God-given armor (Eph.6:11-17), and **stand** unafraid in the face of our relentless foe, deflecting his flaming arrows with the shield of <u>faith</u>, a faith that knows God and believes that *Satan cannot get the advantage over us* (1 John 5:4; 2 Cor.2:11) *as long as:*

1) we are standing in Christ's <u>righteousness</u>, and not our own;
2) we are living in and obedient to the <u>truth</u> of Jesus, the Word; 3) by the <u>salvation</u> of God (Acts 28:28) our minds have been renewed through repentance and forgiveness of sins;
4) we let <u>the Holy Spirit</u> teach us <u>the Word</u>, and how to use it to resist the devil;
5) we are <u>ready to share the Gospel of peace</u> wherever we go.

The book of Revelation has a lot to say about the rewards Jesus will give to overcomers (Rev.2:7, 11, 17, 26; 3:5, 12, 21; 21:7). Be encouraged to walk in the victory that is yours in Christ! .

37

GOD'S GIFTS FOR THE TRAVELERS

"E very good gift and every perfect gift is from above, and comes down from the Father of lights" (Jas.1:17). "Now concerning *spiritual gifts*, ..., I do not want you to be ignorant"; "There are diversities of gifts, but the same Spirit"; "the *manifestation of the Spirit* is <u>given to each one</u> **for the profit of all**"; distributing to each one individually as He wills" (1 Cor.12:1, 4, 7, 11). Note: For this study we will focus only on <u>the gifts of the Spirit</u> to individual believers, which are often referred to as the *manifestation* gifts (v.7-10). In Acts 1:8 Jesus said "You shall receive *power* when the Holy Spirit has come upon you." Remember, this is referring to the *baptism* in the Holy Spirit, anointing us for ministry. The power that we receive by this baptism is *made evident* (*manifested*) through the gifts, because each gift is a <u>supernatural ability</u>, (not a 'sanctified natural ability'). As we operate in the power of the Spirit, He gives us the required gift for <u>a particular occasion</u>, "as He wills", not to put emphasis on the gift, or on our giftedness, but <u>to show His power</u>, and <u>to enable us to minister</u> to others effectively. I would venture to say that the inability of the body

of Christ to minister to the members of the body in contemporary churches, and the lack of outreach through spiritual ministry, is because the Biblical teaching on the baptism in the Spirit, and the resultant gifting by the Spirit, has been scratched off the menu of our necessary food. We've been fattened on milk, but rendered weak and puny because we have not had the power-building meat required for spiritual growth and maturity (Heb.5:12-14; 6:1-2). We are trying to live the spiritual life without the spiritual power, and have remained babies attached to the bottle (1 Pet.2:2), wanting to be spoon-fed on pureed food, instead of warriors engaged in the battle, chewing on the hard-to-digest meat of God's word! (1 Cor.3:1-3; 2 Pet.3:18; Eph.4:11-16; 6:10-13) It is time to move on towards maturity (Phil.4:13-16).

The nine gifts listed in 1 Cor.12:8-10, which comprise the complete manifestation of the Holy Spirit's power, were fully evident in the life of Jesus, the perfect Son of man (John 3:34). In those of us who are less than perfect - not so much. Perhaps this is because our faith is "measured out to us" (Rom.12:3), or to prevent us from being "exalted above measure" (2 Cor.12:7). Just a thought! In any case, we need to remember that not all of us have every gift (1 Cor.12:29-30). We are encouraged to desire these gifts, especially prophecy (1 Cor.12:31; 14:1), but ultimately it is God who sees the heart, and knows if we are ready to receive. And asking for the gifts comes with a proviso: Without the fruit of the Spirit (love, and its components – Gal.5:22-23; Rom.5:5), the gifts of the Spirit are null and void (1 Cor.13). In our desire for the gifts of the Spirit, we must never try to create them or imitate them ourselves. Just as we cannot fake love (the fruit), <u>we cannot fake the gifts</u>. If we try, we deceive ourselves, do harm rather than good, and bring dishonor to God. Another truth to remember, we cannot be a true minister for Christ without the baptism of His Spirit for power (Acts 1:4-8; 2:1-4ff.), and

172

neither can we be a minister of His gifts without His power and love. God gives us the spiritual gift(s) according to what He sees we need and will use for the ministry He has led us into, for the building up of the body of Christ; and to show His power and love to His children, and to those who will believe as a result (1 Cor.14:3, 12, 24-26).

I am struck by the brevity of the presentation here in Paul's first letter to the Corinthian believers – just a simple mention of each gift, with absolutely no definition or explanation, except an emphasis on the fact that they are all from the Spirit of God, and though seemingly distributed at random, are given at His will and discretion. The only ones that get much further attention are the gift of prophecy (with some good press) and the gift of tongues (with some not-so-favorable comments) (1 Cor.14). I noted in this same chapter that prophecy is for believers, and tongues is a sign for unbelievers (1 Cor. 14:22). Also, that Paul laid down rules around the tongue gift in order to prevent confusion. So I am left to wonder if the other gifts are self-explanatory; or if there are any number of possibilities, so that no one can claim a certain word or miracle as being more legitimate than another. Or, perhaps, because they are *spiritual* gifts, they cannot be defined with our mortal, finite thinking! Truth be told, <u>none of them can be adequately described or explained</u>.

Put simply, a <u>word of wisdom</u> is a message spoken to a person or a group, which through supernatural revelation brings clarity and solution concerning a certain situation or problem. A <u>word of knowledge</u> is also a divine revelation in the spirit, where without any prior knowledge, something about a person or a situation is spoken, so it is obvious that it is beyond the natural. This may be in regards to a person's health, needs or concerns, etc. Pretty hard to explain that to your ordinary man on the street! The third gift on the list is <u>faith</u>. God gives some people extraordinary faith that believes God for supernatural answers to specific prayer, without any doubts that they will receive exactly what they ask for. It is few people to whom God gives this gift of extra large faith!

Notice that mention is next made of gifts of healing – not *the* gift, as in *one*, but suggesting that there are different ways in which healing is ministered, and it involves the Spirit's supernatural healing of the body, soul and spirit, bringing shalom to the whole person (3 John 2; Isa.53:4-5). The working of miracles is a divine enabling to do something outside of the natural realm, and may include creative miracles to replace organs or defective body parts. The gift of prophecy, the one most to be desired, is a revelation from the Spirit (usually sudden) to *comfort*, *exhort* or *encourage* someone (1Cor.14:3). This is *not the same* as being a prophet in the sense of foretelling future events.

Discerning of spirits is a gift we could all use, even in the simple sense of knowing how to recognize the voice or thoughts of the Holy Spirit, as opposed to the lies, accusations and condemnation of the evil one. As we operate in the authority we have been given to cast out evil spirits in the name of Jesus, the gift of discerning of spirits is given so that the spirits can be cast out by name i.e. spirits of fear, bitterness, accusation, the occult, witchcraft, etc. The gift of tongues often accompanies the baptism in the Holy Spirit (Acts 2:4), and can be used in private to renew us in our spirit (Jude 20; Eph.6:18; 1 Cor.14:14-15). If used as a sign to unbelievers, it is to be interpreted by someone with the gift of interpretation of tongues who can relay the meaning of the message to the hearers.

Desire these special gifts, and use them to minister in love to fellow travelers on or off the High Way!

38

"MANY WILL SEE IT"

𝕏

*V*erse three of our key text in Psa.40 says that "Many will see it and fear, and will trust in the LORD." What is it they will see? Will they notice that we've been brought up out of a horrible pit, out of the miry clay? Will they see that we are walking with firm and guided steps along a solid pathway, and that we sing as we go? Perhaps. But maybe it is no coincidence that the words "Praise to our God" immediately precede "Many will see it". As mentioned in chapter four, our entire lives should be an expression of praise / worship to God (1 Pet.2:9). Unless we are cloistered hermits, the way we live, talk and act will be seen by everyone we have contact with. The Hebrew word translated 'see' here has numerous applications, and might have been rendered 'behold', 'regard', 'notice', 'consider', 'have respect', etc. Is my life, and is your life noticed, because we are different from the norm? Does our light shine before men, so that they see our good works and glorify God as a result? (Matt.5:14-16) Do our lives agree with the witness we speak with our lips? Is our life alone a witness of God's love, even if we never speak of it?

Acts 2:42-47 records that fear came on everyone who saw the changed lives of the first believers in Jerusalem at Pentecost, and the wonders and signs that followed the Apostles. Notice was taken of the love and care they had for each other; their unity and fellowship; their joy and sincerity. They were continually "praising God, and having favor with all the people". And what happened as a result? Every day, more people believed, and became part of God's family! The people at the temple gate saw a man walking, leaping and praising God, and knowing it was the lame man who had sat and begged there for years, "were filled with wonder and amazement at what had happened to him" (Acts 3:1-10). According to 2 Cor.5:17, "If anyone is in Christ, he is a new creation; old things have passed away; behold, all things have become new". The difference in our lives should make people notice and wonder. Does the world "know we are Christians by our love"? (John 13:34-35) If they witnessed in us today what was evident in the lives of those early believers, our churches would burst at the seams, and house churches would probably spring up in huge numbers. We, like them, would "turn the world upside down" (Acts 17:6).

As we journey along this High Way of Life, individually, as well as corporately we are being observed by many who are not on the same path. Do they fear and turn to the Lord as they see the praise of our lives, or do they scorn and ridicule the sham and hypocrisy of our lives? Do we display "love, joy, peace, patience, kindness, gentleness, goodness, faithfulness and self-control"? (Gal.5:22-23) Or are we a picture of hate, gloom, anxiety, impatience, criticism, rudeness, evil speech, unreliability, greed, anger etc.? Are they attracted to the Christ in us or repulsed by our likeness to them? (1 Pet.3:3-4; 2 Cor.2:15; 1 Pet.2:11-12) Do they see as many hurting, sick, poor and depressed people among us, as they see on the streets of any city? Or do they see miracles of healing and restored lives, and that we love and minister to each other as members of the body? (Rom.12; 1 Cor.12, 13)

One of my aims and purposes in writing this book was to show people (namely God's children) how they can get 'unstuck' from the hurts of the past, and iniquities of the generations. God has allowed me to witness firsthand glazed, lifeless eyes disappear, and instantly be replaced with eyes that sparkle with light, when a spirit of occultism was cast out in the name of Jesus. I have seen healing in body, soul and spirit, when the evil spirits of un-forgiveness, bitterness, rejection, etc. were also evicted by the power of that Name. I am living, walking proof of amazing transformation in my life, renewal of my mind and healing of my soul and body. I hold no anger against those who withheld this teaching from me, and from hundreds of others over the years, leaders who ignored the teaching of the Holy Spirit baptism and gifts, and dismissed them as heretical or not for today. I do feel incredible sadness as I think about it, because as a result Satan has had far too much control over so many believers who have not known they can be delivered from his tyranny (The fact of spiritual warfare has been neglected in the teaching of many pastors and churches as well). The anger I have is toward our arch enemy, the devil, who has wreaked such horrific havoc in people's lives, and held them in bondage and torment for decades; and they have had no one in the church (in most cases) who could help them get free, because of blinded eyes among the leaders.

I challenge pastors and Bible teachers to look at the Word of God with eyes enlightened by the Holy Spirit (John 16:13); to let the Word say what it says, not what the church fathers over the centuries have decided it says (1 Cor.2:4-5; 3:19-21; 2 Cor.4:2); to be willing to repent of fundamentalist legalism, with its traditions and doctrines of men (Col.2:20-

23; Gal.5:1); and to begin to teach the whole counsel of God, as Paul did (Acts 20:26-27). I plead with those who pander to market demands (2 Tim.4:3-4), with a watered-down version of the Gospel, which is no Gospel at all, to return to the teaching of the cross (1 Cor.2:2) and repentance of sin (2 Cor.7:10; 2 Tim.2:24-26); of sanctification, holiness, and purity (Eph.1:4; 5:25-27; 1 Pet.1:15-16; 1 John 3:3); of obedience (John 14:15; Rom.6:12-13) and of lives yielded to God's will (Rom.12:1-2); of spiritual warfare (2 Cor.10:4-5; Eph.6:12); and of the Holy Spirit (Rom.8; Gal.3:3). Lead your people in the supernatural power and wisdom of the Holy Spirit, not in the futile thinking of man's understanding (1 Cor.2:12-13). Your people will experience a new shalom (well-being) in spirit, soul and body; and the body of Christ will be nurtured and built up in love and the unity of the Spirit, in the bond of peace (3 John 2; Eph.4:3-4; 1 Cor.12:7-11; Acts 1:8). There will be some who aren't comfortable with this new look, and will leave. But thirsty, needy hearts, who are seeking truth and a change in their lives, will be drawn in, as Jesus is lifted up, and lives are transformed (John 7:37-39; Rev.22:17; Matt.11:28-30). The light will attract them and point them to Christ (Matt.5:16), and the love will draw them to take refuge in the cross of Christ (Heb.6:18-19).

If you think this is just alarmist, and unnecessary prattle, please take a few moments to read the letters of Jesus to the churches, recorded in Rev.2 and 3. Especially note Rev.2:5. As many churches around the world are already aware, persecution separates the wheat from the chaff, the genuine believer from the pretender. Before it comes to that, give glory to God and be led, not by the spirit of mammon, but by the Spirit of God, to let the sifting begin as Truth is taught. Start by preaching and practicing the words of 2 Chron.7:14. We need to stop "playing church", wake out of our sleep and let our light shine (Phil.2:15)!

39

A HOMECOMING SONG

🌸

*D*id you ever wonder what the disciples thought when Jesus suddenly announced *"In my Father's house are many mansions. I go to prepare a place for you, and I will come and receive you to myself, that where I am, there you may be also"*? (John 14:1-3) It must have been music to the ears of the twelve who had been living as nomads for three years, and were facing separation from their dear friend in a short time. Jesus' simple words still thrill our hearts today. You see, when we were born again into God's family, we immediately received a new life, and our 'citizenship papers' for heaven (Eph.2:19; Phil.3:20), signed, sealed and delivered by the Holy Spirit (Rom.8:15-17; 2 Cor.1:22; Eph.1:13-14; 4:30). He has placed in our hearts a longing for our new home, to "be forever with the Lord" (1 Thes.4:16-17), the One who is our Savior, Shepherd, and Bridegroom. I think of wives and children who have been left behind while the husband and father goes away to prepare a home for them in a new land. What a day of rejoicing when they are all together in their new home!

John Bunyan's classic "The Pilgrim's Progress" takes us on an allegorical journey with Christian, from his new birth in

179

Christ, to the final triumphal entrance into His Lord's presence, with many trials and joys along the way. The experiences of this believer may not all happen to all of us, but the same hope and expectation keeps us "pressing on the upward way". John Bunyan, himself, writing from a jail cell in England, no doubt often yearned for 'home' even as he penned the words that still speak today, over four hundred years later. No doubt as he thought about heaven, his heart was filled with song, and the dank, dark, dirty cells and corridors of his prison reverberated with the melody of joy and hope that poured from his lips.

The word 'pilgrimage' was used by Jacob to describe his life, and those of his forefathers (Gen.47:9), who had lived in tents, as strangers and sojourners while awaiting possession of Canaan (Exod.6:4), the Promised Land. David also compares his life to a pilgrimage (Psa.119:54). Hebrews describes Old Testament believers as "strangers and pilgrims on the earth", who in faith believed God's promises and sought a homeland in heaven, in a city prepared for them by God! (Heb.11:13-16) Building on this idea, he shows how much better our position is today, through Christ, who mediated the new covenant. Through faith in Him we have inherited those promises, and are partakers now in the blessings they could only dream of, even while we are on the journey home (Heb.11:39-40; 12:22-24). Heb.12:28 affirms how unshakable and firm our inherited kingdom is, and admonishes us therefore to serve God acceptably, with grace, reverence and godly fear. This message to us pilgrims is reiterated in 1 Pet.2:11-12. As citizens of the kingdom of light, we are to walk in the light, behaving as people of the kingdom of heaven, and not as citizens of the world of darkness. We need to be reminded frequently that we already have eternal life, because we have God's life in us, by His Spirit, and are already seated in heaven with Him (Eph.2:6;

Col.3:1-3). So we are to lay up treasures in heaven, rather than on earth (Matt.6:19-21), and to set our mind on things above (Col.3:1-2).

In the best sense of the word, 'home' is a very comforting place. You feel safe, loved, at ease. Things are familiar. You can be 'yourself'. You are happy because you are among family. Some of you may never have experienced a home like this – it may be nothing more than a fantasy of your wistful imagination. Perhaps you can't even picture such a place in your mind, because nothing in your experience can relate to it. I've often tried to understand what heaven, our future home as believers, will be like. As I was growing up, there was a plethora of Gospel songs on the theme of heaven, and many of them may not have been exactly a true portrayal of what John saw in his revelation. I have a feeling that he didn't have the physical senses needed to take it all in, or the language to adequately describe it. Shall we 'sneak a peek'? (to borrow a phrase from the Calgary Stampede pre-opening night).

Look at John's description of Jesus (Rev.1:13-18; 19:11-16) and those who praised Him (5:2-14; 14:1-5; 15:2-4); and of God and those who worshiped Him (4:2-11; 11:16-19). John saw great multitudes of believers (7:9-15; 14:1-5; 19:1-9); plus thrones and judgments (20:4, 11-15). Finally he 'saw' a new heaven, a new earth (21:1), and the New Jerusalem (21:2, 9-27; 22:1-5). If you have read these verses, you realize it's pretty hard to fathom what our new home will be like – our finite minds just cannot grasp its magnitude or splendor. What we can understand, and look forward to, are the simple truths of 7:16-17 – no more hunger, thirst or tears; 21:4 – no sorrow, pain or death; 21:25 – no night; 21:8, 27 – no evil or defilement of any kind. This in itself should provide us with song lyrics that the world does not comprehend and cannot sing. But the overriding theme of our songs of home will be the One who came to seek and to save the lost (Luke 19:10); who left the purity of heaven, laying aside His deity (Phil.2:6-8) to live as a mortal in a sin-cursed world, in order to deliver us from the kingdom of darkness into the kingdom of light (1 Pet.2:9); who died a horrendous death to give us marvelous, abundant life (John 3:16; 10:10b-11)); who took all our sins, sorrows and sickness upon Himself on the cross that we might be saved and healed (Isa.53:4-6), and so that we could have His righteousness on us (2 Cor.5:21; Rom.3:21-22).

All the songs we have been singing along the pilgrim journey will be a part of the homecoming song of jubilation and celebration. We will continue to lift up our praise to the Lamb who sits on His throne (Rev.5:8-13), and to the God who loved us and chose us before the foundation of the earth (Eph.1:4; Rev.15:3-4). We will never tire of singing of His measureless Father-love (1 John 3:1). Our hearts will swell with praise and thanksgiving as we sing the song of redemption and deliverance; and the angels will listen in wonder to this song they cannot sing, because they have never experienced this amazing grace of God (1 Pet.1:10-12). The peace and joy that flooded our hearts and sustained us through the trials of our earthly life, will permeate every particle of whatever makes up the fabric of heaven, including our praise (Psa.16:11), so the songs will continue to flow. And of course we will include in our salvation symphony the victory anthem, in honor of the One who triumphed over sin and death and hell, and ultimately over the great initiator and perpetrator of these, and of all evil; whom we have overcome by the blood of the Lamb, and in His powerful Name, which is above every name. All praise will be given to the 'Homecoming King', the King of kings and Lord of lords, who is celebrating the welcoming home of His beautiful bride, the Church, for whom He died and rose again. To Him be praise and honor and glory forever and ever! AMEN!!

CPSIA information can be obtained at www.ICGtesting.com
Printed in the USA
LVOW102139161112

307553LV00002B/1/P